PreMBA Analytical Primer

PreMBA Analytical Primer

Essential Quantitative Concepts for Business Math

Regina Treviño

PREMBA ANALYTICAL PRIMER

First published in 2008 by
PALGRAVE MACMILLAN®
in the United States—a division of St. Martin's Press LLC,
175 Fifth Avenue, New York, NY 10010.

Where this book is distributed in the UK, Europe and the rest of the world,
this is by Palgrave Macmillan, a division of Macmillan Publishers Limited,
registered in England, company number 785998, of Houndmills,
Basingstoke, Hampshire RG21 6XS.

Palgrave Macmillan is the global academic imprint of the above companies
and has companies and representatives throughout the world.

Palgrave® and Macmillan® are registered trademarks in the United States,
the United Kingdom, Europe and other countries.

ISBN-13: 978-0-230-60912-9 (hardcover)
ISBN-10: 0-230-60912-0 (hardcover)
ISBN-13: 978-0-230-60913-6 (paperback)
ISBN-10: 0-230-60913-9 (paperback)

Library of Congress Cataloging-in-Publication Data

Trevino, Regina.
    PreMBA analytical primer : essential quantitative concepts for business
math / Regina Trevino.
        p. cm.
    Includes bibliographical references and index.
    ISBN 0-230-60913-9
        1. Business mathematics. 2. Investments—Mathematics. I. Title.

HF5691.T74 2008
650.01'513—dc22   2008006209

A catalogue record of the book is available from the British Library.

Design by Newgen Imaging Systems (P) Ltd., Chennai, India.

First edition: October 2008

10 9 8 7 6 5 4 3 2 1

Printed in the United States of America.

a mi esposo Paul

CONTENTS

Preface   xi

Mathematical Symbols and Abbreviations   xiii

1   Business Math: Functions and Graphs   1
    1.1   Functions   1
        Application 1.1   The Revenue Function   2
        1.1.1   Multivariate Functions   3
        Application 1.2   The Demand and Supply Functions   3
    1.2   Graphing Functions   4
        Application 1.3   The Demand Curve   5
    1.3   Equations   7
    1.4   Linear Functions   7
        1.4.1   Solving Linear Equations   8
        Application 1.4   Linear Demand Curves   9
        1.4.2   Solving Linear Inequalities   10
    1.5   Slopes and Intercepts of Linear Equations   12
        1.5.1   Slope-Intercept Form of a Line   13
        Application 1.5   Graphing a Linear Demand Curve   17
        1.5.2   Finding the Equation of a Line   19
        1.5.3   General Linear Form of a Line   20
        Application 1.6   The Consumer's Budget Constraint   21
        1.5.4   Horizontal and Vertical Lines   25
    1.6   Solving Two-Variable Systems of Linear Equations   26
        Application 1.7   Market Equilibrium   27
    1.7   Properties of Functions   30
        Application 1.8   Kinked Budget Constraints   31
    1.8   Exponents   33
        Application 1.9   Cobb-Douglas Production Function   33
        1.8.1   Radicals and Fractional Exponents   34
        1.8.2   Homogenous Functions   35
        Application 1.10   Constant Returns to Scale   35
    1.9   Changes and Growth Rates   36
        1.9.1   Growth Rate Formulas   37
        Application 1.11   The Sources of Economic Growth   38

	1.9.2 Index Numbers	39
	Application 1.12 Consumer Price Index and Inflation	39
	Practice Exercises	40
2	**Business Math: Optimization**	**45**
	2.1 Nonlinear Functions	45
	2.2 The Concept of a Derivative	45
	2.2.1 Notation of Derivatives	47
	2.2.2 Rules of Differentiation	47
	Application 2.1 Marginal Functions	49
	2.3 Graphical Interpretation of Derivatives	50
	Application 2.2 Marginal Product of Labor	52
	2.4 Additional Topics on Derivatives	54
	2.5 Second Derivatives	55
	Application 2.3 Diminishing Marginal Utility	57
	2.6 Partial Derivatives	59
	Application 2.4 Partial Derivatives and the Ceteris Paribus Assumption	60
	Application 2.5 Income Elasticity of Demand	60
	2.7 Optimization	61
	2.7.1 Unconstrained Optimization	62
	Application 2.6 Profit Maximization	64
	2.7.2 Constrained Optimization	66
	Application 2.7 Consumer's Utility Maximization Problem	67
	2.8 Exponential and Logarithmic Functions	69
	Application 2.8 Continuously Compounded Interest Rate	70
	2.8.1 Logarithmic Functions	71
	2.8.2 The Natural Logarithm	71
	Application 2.9 Doubling Time for an Investment	72
	2.8.3 Differentiation of e and ln	73
	2.9 Measuring Areas under Linear Functions	73
	Application 2.10 Consumer Surplus	74
	2.10 Economic Models	76
	2.10.1 Flow and Stock Variables	77
	Application 2.11 Balance Sheet and Income Statement	77
	2.10.2 Nominal and Real Economic Variables	77
	Application 2.12 Nominal and Real GDP	77
	2.11 Comparative Statics Analysis	79
	Application 2.13 Shifting the Demand and Supply Curves	79
	Practice Exercises	81
3	**Statistical Analysis Primer**	**83**
	3.1 Elements of Statistics	83
	3.2 Sigma Notation	84

3.3	Measures of Central Tendency	85
3.4	Frequency Tables and Histograms	87
3.5	Measures of Variability	92
3.6	Measures of Association	93
3.7	Probability Essentials	97
3.8	Discrete Random Variables	98
	3.8.1 Discrete Random Variables and Expected Value	100
	3.8.2 Discrete Random Variables and Variance	101
	3.8.3 Decision Tree Basics	103
3.9	Continuous Random Variables	106
	3.9.1 The Normal Distribution	107
	3.9.2 Standardizing: z-Values	108
	3.9.3 Standard Normal Tables and z-Values	108
3.10	An Introduction to Estimation	112
	3.10.1 The Sampling Distribution of the Sample Mean	113
3.11	Regression Analysis	115
	3.11.1 Simple Linear Regression	115
3.12	Hypothesis Testing	121
	3.12.1 Types of Errors	121
	3.12.2 Significance from p-Values	122
	Practice Exercises	124
4	Mathematics of Finance	131
4.1	Time Value of Money	131
	4.1.1 Present Value	132
	4.1.2 Future Value	133
4.2	Nominal and Real Rates of Interest	134
4.3	Compound Interest	135
	4.3.1 Continuous Compounding	136
	4.3.2 Effective Interest Rate	137
4.4	Annuities	139
	4.4.1 Amortization of Loans	139
4.5	Perpetuities	140
	4.5.1 Growing Perpetuities	142
4.6	Net Present Value	143
	4.6.1 Discounted Cash Flow	144
	4.6.2 Risk-Adjusted Discount Rates	145
4.7	Bonds	146
	4.7.1 Zero-Coupon Bonds	148
4.8	Common Stocks	149
4.9	Portfolio Theory Primer	150

4.9.1	Portfolio Math	150
4.9.2	Diversification and Portfolio Risk	154
4.9.3	Measuring Risk	155
Practice Exercises		158

Appendix A: List of Rules — 163

Appendix B: Answers to Practice Exercises — 169

Notes — 193

References — 197

Index — 199

PREFACE

This book is a review of the analytical methods required in most of the quantitative courses taught at MBA programs. Students with no technical background, or who have not studied mathematics since college, may easily feel overwhelmed by the mathematical formalism that is typical of quantitative courses, such as economics, statistics, or finance. These students will benefit from a concise and focused review of the analytical tools that will become a necessary skill in their MBA classes. The objective of this book is to present the essential quantitative concepts and methods in a self-contained, nontechnical, and intuitive way.

I divide the contents of the book into three broad sections: business math, statistics, and finance. In the business math section (chapters 1 and 2), each analytical method is followed by an application that illustrates how such tool is typically used in MBA quantitative courses. In these applications, wherever possible, I provide the background and context to facilitate understanding and stimulate interest.

Chapter 3 is a statistical analysis primer and chapter 4 is a review of the mathematics of finance. The topics covered in both these chapters represent a knowledge basis that is essential before taking any MBA statistics, operations research, and finance courses. Simple examples are used to illustrate the topics covered in chapters 3 and 4.

THE STYLE OF THE BOOK

In choosing the contents of *PreMBA Analytical Primer: Essential Quantitative Concepts for Business Math*, I tried to err on the side of inclusion. My aim is to assure coverage of most of the analytical tools that students may be required to handle during their MBA courses.

I sought a style of presentation that is accessible yet rigorous. Wherever possible, I give precise definitions of the concepts covered. At the same time, I accompany this analysis with examples that illustrate the key points.

Topics that I consider either relatively advanced or too peripheral are marked with an asterisk (*). This allows students to skip them over easily in a first reading.

How To Use This Book

This book is intended to be a math refresher that serves students both as a primer, and as a reference along their courses. Students with little technical background will benefit from reading and working on the entire book before the start of their MBA classes. Others students, however, might use it as a reference tool for the review of particular topics on a need basis throughout their MBA courses.

The chapters have been written to be relatively self-contained. As a result, a student can alter the sequence in which the different topics (math, statistics, and finance) are reviewed. At the end of the book, I provide a listing with all the major rules covered in the chapters and I also include a brief summary of some basic algebra rules.

I include exercises that test students' understanding of the topics throughout the text as well as a set of practice problems at the end of each chapter. Working through as many of these exercises as possible is the surest way to master the material covered in each chapter. The answers to all the test-your-understanding exercises and practice problems are included at the end of the book.

Acknowledgments

I am very grateful for the constructive comments, advice, and support from my colleagues and friends Bo Becker, Luis Garicano, Tapio Pekkala, Luis Rayo, Lars Stole, and especially, Mine Cinar. I would also like to acknowledge the efforts of my students Dong Li and Jerry Wang, who proofread the entire manuscript.

It was a pleasure to work with everyone at Palgrave Macmillan. My acquisitions editor, Laurie Harting, was a source of excellent advice. Erin Ivy, my production editor, did a sterling job and so did Maran Elancheran and his crew at New Imaging Systems.

Finally, I would like to thank my family, especially my husband Paul, for their loving support and patience during the late nights that I spent working on this project.

Mathematical Symbols and Abbreviations

The use of symbols and notation is explained in a self-contained discussion wherever these appear in each chapter, but for convenience I also list here the major symbol conventions that recur throughout the book.

Symbol	Meaning
Δ	Greek letter delta. Denotes change in the value of a variable.
Π	Greek letter pi (uppercase). Denotes firm profits.
Σ	Greek letter sigma (uppercase). Denotes summation.
α	Greek letter alpha. Denotes significance level of a test.
β	Greek letter beta. Denotes sensitivity of a security's return to market movements.
ε	Greek letter epsilon. Denotes elasticity (chapter 2). Denotes random error (chapter 3).
λ	Greek letter lambda. Denotes Lagrange multiplier.
π	Greek letter pi (lowercase). Denotes inflation.
μ	Greek letter mu. Denotes mean.
ρ	Greek letter rho. Denotes correlation coefficient.
σ	Greek letter sigma (lowercase). Denotes standard deviation.
A	Generic constant. In a Cobb-Douglas production function, it denotes factor productivity.
a	Generic constant. Typically used to denote the vertical intercept of a line.
b	Generic constant. Typically used to denote the slope of a line.
C	Generic constant. Denotes cash flow (chapter 4).
$C(\cdot)$	Cost function.
cdf	Cumulative distribution function.
CPI	Consumer price index.
CS	Consumer surplus.
d	Generic constant. Next to a variable, it denotes small (infinitesimal) change in the value of the variable.
DCF	Discounted cash flow.
DIV	Dividend.
$E(\cdot)$	Expected value.
$f(\cdot)$	Function.

$f'(\cdot)$	First derivative of the function.
$f''(\cdot)$	Second derivative of the function.
F	Face value.
FOC	First order condition.
FV	Future value.
I	Consumer income.
g	Growth rate.
GDP	Gross domestic product.
K	Capital stock.
L	Labor.
ln	Natural logarithm.
MC	Marginal cost.
MPL	Marginal product of labor.
MU	Marginal utility.
N	Normal distribution.
NPV	Net present value.
p	Price of a good.
p_a	Price of an alternative good.
p_m	Price of the materials used to produce a good.
p_t	Price of technologically related goods.
P	Principal.
pdf	Probability density function.
PV	Present value.
q	Quantity (individual level).
Q	Quantity (market level)
Q^d	Quantity demanded.
Q^s	Quantity supplied.
R	Firm revenue.
r	Interest rate.
r_e	Effective interest rate.
r_f	Risk-free interest rate.
r_{xy}	Sample correlation coefficient between variable x and variable y.
s	Sample standard deviation.
SOC	Second order condition.
t	Index variable for time (chapter 4).
$U(\cdot)$	Utility function.
x	Generic variable. Typically denotes the independent variable.
$\bar{x}$	Sample mean.
y	Generic variable. Typically denotes the dependent variable.
Y	Generic variable. In the aggregate production function, it denotes total output.

| | Absolute value.

∞ Infinity.

∂ Partial derivative.

L(·) Lagrangian.

Asterisks, Hats, and Primes

Asterisks: An asterisk is attached to a variable to denote optimal, equilibrium, or solution quantity (e.g., $x^\star$).

Hats: A hat is attached to a variable to denote predicted value (e.g., $\hat{y}$).

Primes: A prime attached to a function of a single variable denotes first derivative (e.g., $f'(x)$).

A prime attached to a variable, as opposed to a function, denotes a specific value of that variable (e.g., p').

CHAPTER 1

Business Math: Functions and Graphs

An analytical approach to business analysis is one that uses rigorous, logical reasoning. This does not necessarily imply the use of mathematical methods. The language of mathematics, however, helps to communicate rather subtle ideas that would otherwise be difficult to explain using plain English.

Business applications that involve economic, financial, accounting, or statistical analysis often require the understanding of how variables relate to one another. There are three primary ways of expressing relationships among variables: functions, graphs, and tables.

1.1   FUNCTIONS

A **variable** is a letter or a symbol used to represent some unknown quantity. Typically, the letters x and y are used to represent variables. Consider the following examples:

- A lightbulb manufacturer who produces x units has a total cost of production of y dollars.
- A salesperson who sells x number of cars per month receives a monthly commission of y dollars.
- The local pizza place sells an average of y pizzas daily when the price per pizza is x dollars.

All these examples have one thing in common: they express relationships between variables. The concept of a *function* is central to any analysis that involves relationships among various types of variables.

A **function** is a "black box" that takes a numerical input(s) and produces a *unique* number as output. The variable that represents the input is called the **independent variable**. The variable that represents the output is called the **dependent variable**. Typically, the variable x represents the independent variable (e.g., number of cars sold) and the variable y represents the dependent variable (e.g., car sale commission received). To express that the variable y is a function of the variable x we write,

$$y = f(x).$$

The symbol $f(x)$ denotes "function of x" and is read as "f of x." This symbol does not mean f times x.

The statement $y = f(x)$ means that to each number x (input), a unique number y will be assigned (output), following the rule described in f. For example, a function describes a rule like "take each number and add 1" or "take each number and square it" and is written as $y = x + 1$ and $y = x^2$, respectively.

From the relation $y = f(x)$, we know that if the value of x changes, the value of y changes as well. For example, suppose that we have the function $y = f(x) = 2x - 1$ and the value of x is $x = 3$. Given this value of x, the value of y is $y = f(3) = 2(3) - 1 = 5$. Now, if the value of x changes to $x = 7$, we have that the new value for y is $y = f(7) = 2(7) - 1 = 13$.

Examples:

1. Consider the function $y = f(x) = 5x - 4$. If $x = 2$, what is the value of y?

   Solution: $y = f(2) = 5(2) - 4 = 6$.

2. Consider the function $y = f(x) = 60 - 2x^2$. If $x = 5$, what is the value of y?

   Solution: $y = f(5) = 60 - 2(5^2) = 10$.

3. Consider the function $y = f(x) = 20 + 2x$. If $x = -1$, what is the value of y?

   Solution: $y = f(-1) = 20 + 2(-1) = 18$.

Application 1.1   The Revenue Function

Consider a small firm that produces widgets that are sold in the market at a price of $2 per unit. Denote the number of widgets sold by q and the firm's sales revenue by R. Sales revenue is calculated as units sold times price per unit. The relationship that we have here is that R (dependent variable) is a function of q (independent variable). In this particular case, the revenue function is given by

$$R = f(q) = 2q.$$

Now, suppose that during a particular month the firm sells 1,000 widgets, that is, $q = 1,000$. We can calculate the monthly revenue by substituting this particular value of q in the function

$$R = f(1,000) = 2(1,000) = \$2,000.$$

1.1.1 Multivariate Functions

Suppose that the value of the variable y depends not only on the value of x but also on the value of other variables, such as w and z. In this case, we have a **multivariate function**, which is denoted as

$$y = f(x, w, z).$$

Just as before, y is the dependent variable and the independent variables are x, w, and z. If the value of any of the independent variables changes, the value of y changes as well. For example, suppose that we have the function $y = f(x, w, z) = 4x - 3w + 6z$ and the values for the independent variables are $x = 3$, $w = 2$, and $z = 4$. Given these values of x, w, and z, the value of y is $y = f(3, 2, 4) = 4(3) - 3(2) + 6(4) = 30$. Now, suppose that the value of z changes to $z = 1$ and the values of the other independent variables remain unchanged. We have that the new value for y is $y = f(3, 2, 1) = 4(3) - 3(2) + 6(1) = 12$.

Examples:

1. Consider the function $y = f(x, w, z) = 5x + 3w - 2z - 4$. If $x = 2$, $w = 0$, and $z = 1$, what is the value of y?

   Solution: $y = f(2, 0, 1) = 5(2) + 3(0) - 2(1) - 4 = 4$.

2. Consider the function $y = f(x, w) = 30 - 2x + 5w$. If $x = 10$ and $w = -1$, what is the value of y?

   Solution: $y = f(10, -1) = 30 - 2(10) + 5(-1) = 5$.

3. Consider the function $y = f(x, z) = 3z^2 - 20 - x$. If $x = 5$ and $z = 2$, what is the value of y?

   Solution: $y = f(5, 2) = 3(2^2) - 20 - 5 = -13$.

Application 1.2   The Demand and Supply Functions
The *demand* indicates the quantity of a particular good that consumers are willing to purchase. It is determined by the price of the good, the price of the alternative goods, and consumer income.

We can denote the quantity demanded Q^d of a good as

$$Q^d = f(p, p_a, I),$$

where $f(\cdot)$ represents the demand function, p is the price of the good, p_a is the price of alternative goods, and I is income. For example, suppose that a particular good has a demand function given by

$$Q^d = f(p, p_a, I) = 200 - 3p + 4p_a + 2I,$$

and we are told that the price at which the good is sold is $p = \$4$ per unit, that the price of the alternative good is $p_a = \$3$ per unit, and that consumer income is $I = \$100$. To find out how much consumers will purchase of this particular good, we substitute this information in the demand function to get

$$Q^d = f(4, 3, 100) = 200 - 3(4) + 4(3) + 2(100) = 400 \text{ units.}$$

The *supply* indicates the quantity of a particular good that producers are willing to sell. It depends on the price of the good, the price of the materials used to produce the good, and the price of technologically related goods. We can denote the quantity supplied Q^s of a good as

$$Q^s = f(p, p_m, p_t),$$

where $f(\cdot)$ represents the supply function, p_m is the price of the materials used to produce the good (i.e., the price of the inputs of production), and p_t is the price of technologically related goods. For example, suppose that a particular good has a supply function given by

$$Q^s = f(p, p_m, p_t) = 10p - 2p_m - p_t,$$

and we are told that the price at which the good is sold is $p = \$15$ per unit, that the price of the raw material used in production is $p_m = \$10$ per unit, and that the price of a technologically related good is $p_t = \$30$. To find out how much producers will supply of this particular good, we substitute this information in the supply function to get

$$Q^s = f(15, 10, 30) = 10(15) - 2(10) - 30 = 100 \text{ units.}$$

I.2 GRAPHING FUNCTIONS

A **graph** of a function allows us to visualize the relationship between the variables. Graphs are depicted in a two-dimensional space using the **Cartesian plane**. Any pair of real numbers can be identified with a **point** (x, y) in the Cartesian plane, as shown in figure 1.1. When we graph a function, the independent variable is typically depicted on the horizontal axis, often called the **x-axis**, and the dependent variable on the vertical axis, often called the **y-axis**.

The plane is divided into four quadrants depending on whether x and y are positive or negative numbers. In the first quadrant, x and y are both positive

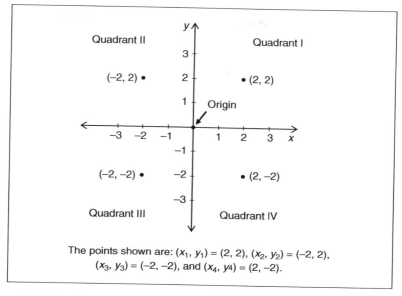

The points shown are: $(x_1, y_1) = (2, 2)$, $(x_2, y_2) = (-2, 2)$, $(x_3, y_3) = (-2, -2)$, and $(x_4, y_4) = (2, -2)$.

Figure 1.1 The Cartesian Plane

numbers. In the second quadrant, x is a negative number and y is a positive number. In the third quadrant, x and y are both negative numbers. Finally, in the fourth quadrant, x is a positive number and y is a negative number. The point of intersection of the axes is called the **origin**, and it corresponds to the point $(x, y) = (0, 0)$.

Suppose that for a particular analysis we wanted to restrict our attention to cases in which the variables x and y assume only nonnegative values (i.e., $x \geq 0$ and $y \geq 0$). In this case, we would typically depict the graph in the first quadrant only. Figure 1.2 illustrates an example of a graph of a function depicted only for nonnegative values of x and y.

In the example of figure 1.2, we can see that there is a *positive relationship* between the value of x and the value of y. That is, as x becomes larger, y becomes larger as well. We will discuss this in more detail when we introduce the concept of *slope*.

Application 1.3   The Demand Curve

The *demand curve* is the graphical representation of the demand function. From our discussion in application 1.2, we know that the demand function for a good is given by

$$Q^d = f(p, p_a, I).$$

It is convenient, however, to graph Q^d simply as a function of its own price, p, with the understanding that the variables p_a and I are being held constant.

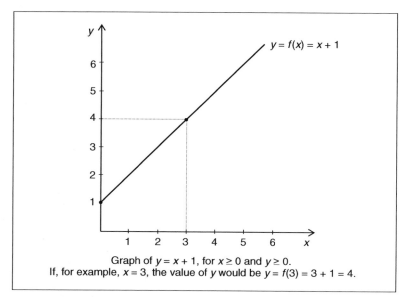

Figure 1.2 Graphing a Function

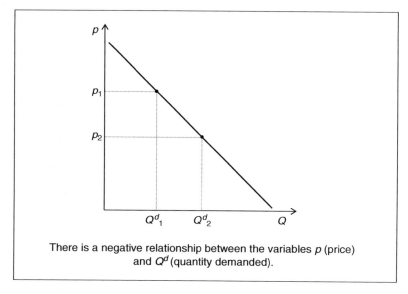

Figure 1.3 Demand Curve

Thus, a demand curve, like that of figure 1.3, shows the relationship between the price of the good and the quantity of the good, assuming all other determinants of the demand remain unchanged. Generally, a higher price for the good, other things equal, leads consumers to demand a smaller quantity of the good. This means that there is a *negative relationship* between the variables p and Q^d. We can see this by looking at the graph. As the variable p (price) becomes smaller, the variable Q^d (quantity demanded) becomes larger.

Note that, for historical rather than good economic reasons, in the demand and supply models, the independent variable, price, is graphed on the vertical axis and the dependent variable, quantity, on the horizontal axis.

1.3 EQUATIONS

Equations of various types are used constantly in business. Companies must determine selling prices, advertising budgets, inventory levels, product mix, and so on. Translating the relationship between the different variables into mathematical symbols facilitates problem-solving and decision making.

An **equation** is a statement that two expressions are equal, for example, $y = x + 1$. The two expressions that make up the equation are called **sides** and they are separated by an equal sign. Typically, we call each side of the equation the **left-hand side** and the **right-hand side**, respectively. In our example, the left-hand side is the variable y and the right-hand side is $x + 1$.

An equation contains **variables**, which are represented with letters, and **constants**, which are numbers. In our example, y and x are variables and the number 1 is a constant. The **terms** of the equation are the variables and constants that form the equation and are typically separated by a plus or minus sign. The right-hand side of the earlier equation, for example, has two terms, x and 1.

The numerical **coefficient** of a variable is the number that multiplies the variable. In the term $3x$, the coefficient of x is 3. If no number is written before the variable, for example, in the term x, then the numerical coefficient is understood to be 1.

The **like terms** of an equation are the terms that contain the same variable and differ only in their numerical coefficients. Like terms can be combined, for example, $3x + 5x$ can be combined to form the single term $8x$.

The **solution** to an equation is the value(s) of the variable(s) that *satisfies* the equation, in other words, that makes the equation true when the variable(s) is substituted by the number(s). The solution to an equation is typically identified with an asterisk, that is, x^*. Figure 1.4 illustrates the use of this terminology with an example.

1.4 LINEAR FUNCTIONS

The function $y = f(x)$ is a **linear function** if it has the form:

$$y = f(x) = a + bx,$$

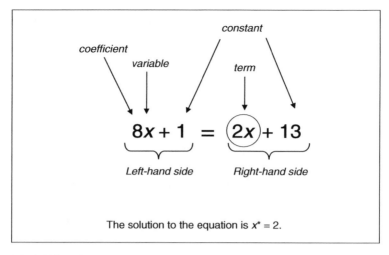

Figure 1.4 Equations

where a and b are constants and $b \neq 0$. The graph of such equation is a straight line.

Linear functions can be expressed **explicitly**, like $y = a + bx$. Here we have an explicit rule that enables us to determine the value of y for each value of x.

Alternatively, linear functions can be expressed **implicitly**, like $ax + by = c$. Here the relationship between the variables x and y is implicitly present. In such cases, we often like to transform the equation to an explicit equation by solving for y in terms of x. We will learn to do this in the next section.

1.4.1 Solving Linear Equations

When solving linear equations, two rules need to be followed (*eq* stands for equation):

RULE 1eq. A term can be moved from one side of an equation to the other if and only if its sign is changed to the opposite sign as it crosses the equal sign.[1]

RULE 2eq. Multiplying or dividing both sides of the equation by the same nonzero number does not alter the equation.

Suppose that we are given an implicit function like

$$ax + by = c,$$

where a, b, and c are constants and $b \neq 0$. If we want to solve the equation for y in terms of x, we proceed as follows:

STEP 1. Start with $ax + by = c$.

STEP 2. Move the term ax to the other side of the equation and change its sign (RULE 1eq), that is, $by = c - ax$.

STEP 3. Divide each term in the equation by b (RULE 2eq), that is, $\frac{by}{b} = \frac{c}{b} - \frac{ax}{b}$. Simplifying, this results in the explicit equation $y = \frac{c}{b} - \frac{a}{b}x$.

Examples:

1. Solve the equation $y - 14 + x = 10 - 2x$ for y in terms of x.
   Solution: $y = 24 - 3x$.

2. Solve the equation $2y - 2x = 10$ for y in terms of x.
   Solution: $y = 5 + x$.

3. Solve the equation $1 + y + 5x = 4y - 2 + 2x$ for y in terms of x.
   Solution: $y = x + 1$.

Application 1.4   Linear Demand Curves

A *linear demand function* has a formula of the form

$$Q^d = a - bp,$$

where a and b are constants larger than zero. If we want to get the *demand curve* or *inverse demand function*, we need to solve the equation for p. The steps are as follows:

STEP 1. Start with $Q^d = a - bp$.

STEP 2. Move the term $-bp$ to the other side of the equation. Remember that you need to change its sign (RULE 1eq). This results in $Q^d + bp = a$.

STEP 3. Move Q^d to the other side, and change its sign as well. This results in $bp = a - Q^d$.

STEP 4. Divide each term of the equation by b (RULE 2eq), that is, $\frac{bp}{b} = \frac{a}{b} - \frac{Q^d}{b}$. Simplifying, this results in $p = \frac{a}{b} - \frac{1}{b}Q^d$, which is the equation of the demand curve.

Example 1.1: A linear demand curve

Suppose that the *demand function* is given by $Q^d = 100 - 4p$, and we want to get the demand curve to graph it (which we will learn how to do below).

What we need to do is simply to solve the equation for p following the steps outlined earlier.

STEP 1. Start with $Q^d = 100 - 4p$.
STEP 2. Move the term $-4p$ to the other side of the equation changing its sign. This results in $Q^d + 4p = 100$.
STEP 3. Move Q^d to the other side changing its sign as well. This results in $4p = 100 - Q^d$.
STEP 4. Divide each term of the equation by 4, that is, $\frac{4p}{4} = \frac{100}{4} - \frac{Q^d}{4}$. Simplifying, this gives us the following demand curve: $p = 25 - \frac{1}{4}Q^d$.

TEST YOUR UNDERSTANDING 1

(1) Suppose the demand function is given by $Q^d = -\frac{1}{2}p + \frac{1}{2}$. Find the demand curve.
(2) Suppose the demand function is given by $Q^d = 6 - \frac{3}{2}p$. Find the demand curve.

(*Solutions are in Appendix B*)

1.4.2 Solving Linear Inequalities

In many business applications, decision makers face certain constraints on the choices available to them. For example, a firm may have a limited advertising budget, a consumer may have a limited income to spend, or an investor may have limited funds. For this type of applications, we need to set up inequalities.

A **linear inequality** in one variable has the form

$$ax + b \leq cx + d \qquad\qquad (1.1)$$

or the form

$$ax + b < cx + d, \qquad\qquad (1.2)$$

where x is the variable and a, b, c, and d are constants. Equation (1.1) is called an inequality and equation (1.2) is a strict inequality.

When solving linear inequalities, the following rules apply (*in* stands for inequality):

RULE 1in. If the same number is added or subtracted from both sides of an inequality, the resulting inequality has the same direction as the original inequality.

For example, if we start with $3 < 7$ and add 2 to both sides, we get $5 < 9$.

RULE 2in. If both sides of an inequality are multiplied or divided by the same *positive* number, the resulting inequality has the same direction as the original inequality.

For example, if we start with $2 < 10$ and multiply both sides by 2, we get $4 < 20$.

RULE 3in. If both sides of an inequality are multiplied or divided by the same *negative* number, the resulting inequality has the reverse direction of the original inequality.

For example, if we start with $2 < 10$ and multiply both sides by -2, we get $-4 > -20$.

Inequalities are often expressed using **interval notation**. For example, the inequality $x \geq 3$ is written in interval notation as $[3, \infty)$ and the inequality $x < 3$ is written as $(-\infty, 3)$.[2] Table 1.1 shows the connection between inequalities and interval notation.

Examples:

1. Find the solution to $3x + 2 \geq x + 8$.

   Solution:

   $2x + 2 \geq 8$ (Following RULE 1in we add $-x$ to both sides),
   $\quad 2x \geq 6$ (Following RULE 1in we add -2 to both sides),
   $\quad\quad x \geq 3$ (Following RULE 2in we divide both sides by 2).

   This solution is written in interval notation as $[3, \infty)$.

2. Find the solution to $3 - 2x \leq 6$.

   Solution:

   $-2x \leq 3$ (Following RULE 1in we add -3 to both sides),
   $\quad x \geq -\frac{3}{2}$ (Following RULE 3in we divide both sides by -2).

   This solution is written in interval notation as $\left[-\frac{3}{2}, \infty\right)$.

Table 1.1 Inequalities and Interval Notation

Interval Notation	Inequality
$[a, b]$	$a \leq x \leq b$
$[a, b)$	$a \leq x < b$
$(a, b]$	$a < x \leq b$
(a, b)	$a < x < b$
$(-\infty, b]$	$x \leq b$
$(-\infty, b)$	$x < b$
$[a, \infty)$	$x \geq a$
(a, ∞)	$x > a$

3. Find the solution to $4x - 12 > 6x$.

Solution:

$-12 > 2x$ (Following RULE 1in we add $-4x$ to both sides),

$-6 > x$ (Following RULE 2in we divide both sides by 2).

This solution is written in interval notation as $(-\infty, -6)$.

1.5 SLOPES AND INTERCEPTS OF LINEAR EQUATIONS

Business is dynamic. Tax rates, interest rates, prices—these are variables constantly changing. How can we estimate the effect of these changes? For example, the price of a bond is a function of the interest rate. If the interest rate goes up, what happens to the price of the bond? The answer lies in understanding the slope and what it measures. In this section, we will review the concept of slope and some of the standard equations of straight lines.

The Greek letter Δ (delta) is typically used to denote change in the value of a variable. Thus, the notation for a change in the value of the variable x is Δx (note that this does not mean Δ times x). If, for example, x changes from x_1 to x_2, then the change in x is expressed as:

$$\Delta x = x_2 - x_1.$$

Suppose then that y is a function of x given by $y = f(x)$. The rate of change of y with respect to x is the ratio of Δy and Δx and is given by the expression:

$$\frac{\Delta y}{\Delta x} = \frac{f(x_2) - f(x_1)}{x_2 - x_1}.$$

This measures how y (dependent variable) changes as x (independent variable) changes. The **slope** of a function is precisely the rate of change of y as x changes, that is,

$$slope = \frac{\Delta y}{\Delta x}.$$

If y increases whenever x increases, then Δy will have the same sign as Δx and the slope of the function is positive. If, on the other hand, y decreases whenever x increases, then Δy and Δx have opposite signs and the slope of the function is negative. A fundamental property of a straight line is that its slope is constant.

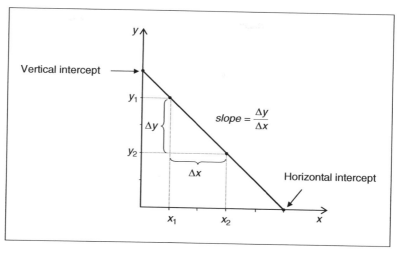

Figure 1.5 Slope and Intercepts with the Axes

The **horizontal intercept** (*x*-intercept) is the point where the graph intersects the horizontal axis (*x*-axis). To find the horizontal intercept, we set $y = 0$ and solve the resulting equation for x.

The **vertical intercept** (*y*-intercept) is the point where the graph intersects the vertical axis (*y*-axis). To find the vertical intercept, we set $x = 0$ and solve the resulting equation for y. Figure 1.5 illustrates our discussion with an example.

1.5.1 Slope–Intercept Form of a Line

The **slope-intercept form** of a line is given by

$$y = a + bx, \tag{1.3}$$

where a and b are constants and $b \neq 0$. This is a useful way of expressing a line since we can immediately identify:

- Slope = b.
- Vertical intercept = a.

Now, let's analyze the components of equation (1.3), that is a and b, in more detail. Our goal is to understand how the graph of the line changes when either of them is varied.

THE SIGN OF b. If b is positive, the line is said to be **upward sloping**. If b is negative, the line is said to be **downward sloping**.

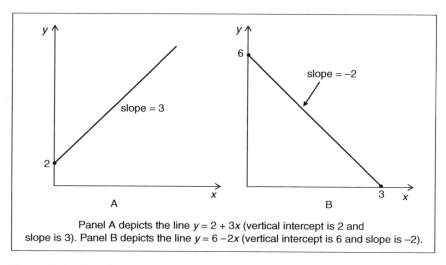

Panel A depicts the line $y = 2 + 3x$ (vertical intercept is 2 and slope is 3). Panel B depicts the line $y = 6 - 2x$ (vertical intercept is 6 and slope is -2).

Figure 1.6 Slope-Intercept Form of a Line

For example, consider the line given by $y = 2 + 3x$. This line has a vertical intercept of 2 and a slope of 3. Panel A in figure 1.6 depicts this line. Now, consider the line given by $y = 6 - 2x$. This line has a vertical intercept of 6 and a slope of -2. Note that we can also find the horizontal intercept, 3 (by substituting $y = 0$ and solving for x). This line is depicted in panel B of figure 1.6.

THE SIZE OF b. The size of the slope, b, affects how fast the function increases (if $b > 0$) or decreases (if $b < 0$). In other words, the magnitude of the slope determines the line's steepness.

To understand the graphical implication of the size of b, let's look at figure 1.7, where we show three lines with the same vertical intercept but different slopes. Panel A compares upward sloping lines (positive slope) and panel B compares downward sloping lines (negative slope). As we can see from these graphs, the larger the *absolute value* of the slope, the steeper the line.[3]

CHANGING a. If the vertical intercept of the line, a, changes, while the slope is unchanged, then the line shifts in or out. Note that since the slope is not changing, this is either an upward or a downward *parallel shift*. Figure 1.8 depicts linear functions that have the same slope but different vertical intercepts.

Progress Exercises

1. Write the slope-intercept formula of a line with a vertical intercept $(0, 3)$ and a slope of 2.

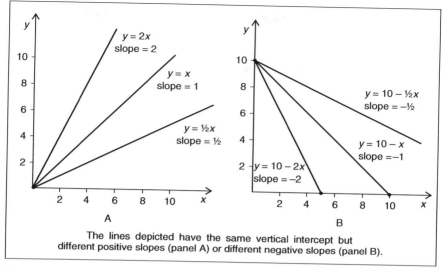

The lines depicted have the same vertical intercept but different positive slopes (panel A) or different negative slopes (panel B).

Figure 1.7 Slopes of Different Sizes

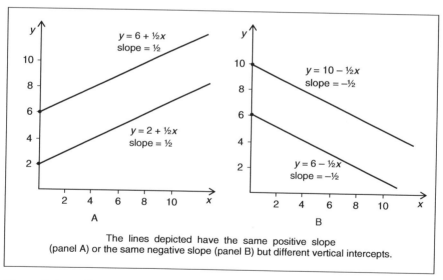

The lines depicted have the same positive slope (panel A) or the same negative slope (panel B) but different vertical intercepts.

Figure 1.8 Different Vertical Intercepts

Solution:

$$y = 3 + 2x$$

2. Write the slope-intercept formula of a line with a vertical intercept $(0, 0)$ and a slope of -3.

Solution:

$y = -3x$

3. Graph the equation $y = 24 - 3x$ (show only the first quadrant of the plane).

Solution:

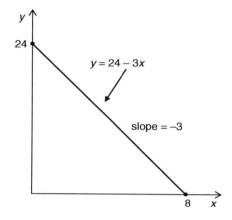

4. Graph the equation $y = 5 + x$ (show only the first quadrant of the plane).

Solution:

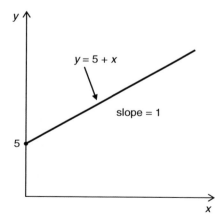

5. Graph the equation $y = 2x + 1$ (show only the first quadrant of the plane).

Solution:

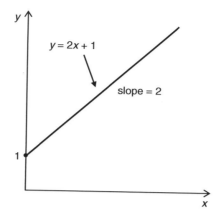

6. Graph the equation $y = 3 - 0.5x$ (show only the first quadrant of the plane).

Solution:

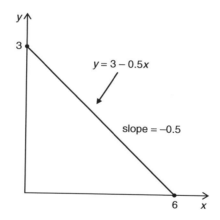

Application 1.5   Graphing a Linear Demand Curve

Suppose that we start with the linear demand curve derived in application 1.4 (for simplicity, we omitted the *d* superscript):

$$p = \frac{a}{b} - \frac{1}{b}Q. \tag{1.4}$$

Equation (1.4) describes a line with a slope of $-\frac{1}{b}$ and a vertical intercept of $\frac{a}{b}$. [We still refer to equation (1.4) as the demand *curve* even though, in this particular case, its graph is a straight line].

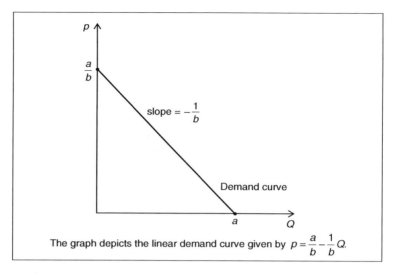

Figure 1.9   Linear Demand Curve

To get the horizontal intercept, we substitute a value of $p = 0$ in equation (1.4) and solve for Q. By doing this, we find that the horizontal intercept is given by the point $(Q, p) = (a, 0)$.

Note that any point (Q, p) that lies on the demand curve will satisfy equation (1.4). Figure 1.9 depicts this linear demand curve.

Example 1.1: A linear demand curve (continued)
Our demand curve is given by (for simplicity, we omitted the d superscript):

$$p = 25 - \frac{1}{4}Q,$$

and we now have enough tools to easily sketch a graph of it.

First, we know that the coefficient of Q, $-\frac{1}{4}$, gives us the slope of the line. This tells us that the line is downward sloping. We can also immediately tell from the equation that the vertical intercept is 25 (i.e., the point $(Q, p) = (0, 25)$).

To get the horizontal intercept, we substitute $p = 0$ and solve the equation for Q. By doing this, we find that the horizontal intercept is given by the point $(Q, p) = (100, 0)$. Figure 1.10 depicts this demand curve.

TEST YOUR UNDERSTANDING 2

(1) Graph the demand curve given by $p = 10 - 0.5Q$.
(2) Suppose the demand function is given by $Q^d = 6 - 2p$. Find the demand curve (i.e., solve the equation for p) and graph it.

(*Solutions are in Appendix B*).

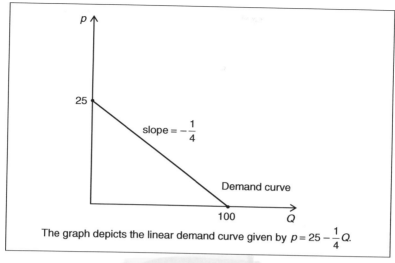

Figure 1.10 Example 1.1 A Linear Demand Curve

1.5.2   Finding the Equation of a Line

Two points determine a straight line. Our objective now is to find the equation of the line, $y = a + bx$, using two points. So, let's assume two distinct points (x_1, y_1) and (x_2, y_2) are given. The formula for the straight line connecting the two points is determined as follows:

STEP 1. Find the slope, b, which is given by

$$b = \frac{\Delta y}{\Delta x} = \frac{y_2 - y_1}{x_2 - x_1}.$$

STEP 2. Now that we have b, let's find the vertical intercept a. To do this, take one of the points, say (x_1, y_1), and plug it into the equation of the line, $y = a + bx$, as follows:

$$y_1 = a + \left(\frac{y_2 - y_1}{x_2 - x_1} \right) x_1.$$

Solving for a we get

$$a = y_1 - \left(\frac{y_2 - y_1}{x_2 - x_1} \right) x_1.$$

Examples:

1. Determine the equation of the line that passes through the points $(2, 5)$ and $(4, 13)$.

Solution:

First, find the slope:

$$b = \frac{y_2 - y_1}{x_2 - x_1} = \frac{13 - 5}{4 - 2} = \frac{8}{2} = 4.$$

Then, find the vertical intercept:

$$a = 5 - (4)\,2 = -3.$$

So, the equation of this line is $y = 4x - 3$.

2. Determine the equation of the line that passes through the points $(1, 7)$ and $(5, 15)$.

Solution:

First, find the slope:

$$b = \frac{y_2 - y_1}{x_2 - x_1} = \frac{15 - 7}{5 - 1} = \frac{8}{4} = 2.$$

Then, find the vertical intercept:

$$a = 7 - (2)\,1 = 5.$$

So, the equation of this line is $y = 2x + 5$.

3. Determine the equation of the line that passes through the points $(1, 8)$ and $(5, 0)$.[4]

Solution:

First, find the slope:

$$b = \frac{y_2 - y_1}{x_2 - x_1} = \frac{0 - 8}{5 - 1} = \frac{-8}{4} = -2.$$

Then, find the vertical intercept:

$$a = 8 - (-2)\,1 = 10.$$

So, the equation of this line is $y = -2x + 10$.

1.5.3 General Linear Form of a Line

The **general linear form** of a line is given by:

$$Ax + Bz = C, \tag{1.5}$$

where A, B, and C are constants and A and B are not both zero. Note that this time, we chose to use the variable z (instead of y). The reason is that

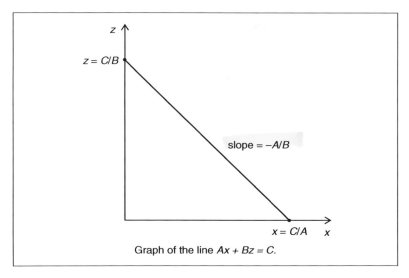

Graph of the line $Ax + Bz = C$.

Figure 1.11 General Linear Form

we want to allow for the case in which there is no dependency between the variables x and z (i.e., here z may not be a function of x).

When we have no information about the relationship (i.e., dependency), if any, between the variables x and z, we can choose to graph the variables on either axis. Suppose that we put the variable x on the horizontal axis and the variable z on the vertical axis. Then, the horizontal intercept is $x = \frac{C}{A}$ (value of x when $z = 0$) and the vertical intercept is $z = \frac{C}{B}$ (value of z when $x = 0$). The slope of this line is $-\frac{A}{B}$. Figure 1.11 depicts this line for the case where A, B, and C are larger than zero.

Now, suppose that the constant C of equation (1.5) increases to C'. This will shift the line outward in a parallel fashion (the slope is not changing). Figure 1.12 depicts this shift. Note that the vertical and horizontal intercepts will both be larger numbers now since the numerator of the fraction increased and the denominator is unchanged.[5] If we had considered a decrease in C, the line would shift inward in a parallel way.

Application 1.6 The Consumer's Budget Constraint
Suppose that a consumer has a certain amount of money, I, to allocate toward the consumption of two goods, good x and good z. The price per unit of good x is p_x and the price per unit of good z is p_z. A *consumption basket*, (x, z), is a list of two numbers that indicates the consumer's chosen amount of each good.

The consumer's *budget constraint* can be written as:

$$p_x x + p_z z = I,$$

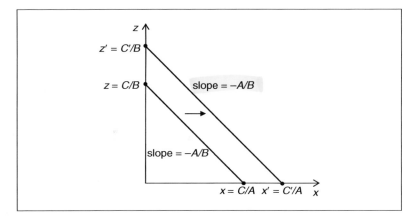

Figure 1.12 General Linear Form

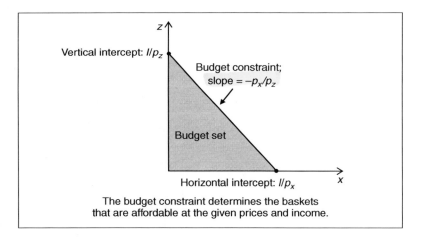

Figure 1.13 The Budget Constraint

where $p_x x$ is the amount of money the consumer is spending on good x and $p_z z$ is the amount of money the consumer is spending on good z. This budget constraint can be graphed as a line. The *affordable consumption baskets*, those that do not cost more than I, are the baskets inside and along the line. These baskets constitute the consumer's *budget set*.

Figure 1.13 depicts the budget constraint graphically. The intercepts with the axes represent the maximum amount of each good that the consumer could purchase if she devoted her entire income exclusively to the consumption of that good.

Example 1.2: Joe's budget constraint

Joe, a freshman in college, receives a monthly allowance of $500 that he needs to allocate toward his consumption of books and food. The price of books is $25 per book and the price of food is $10 per meal. The equation that describes Joe's monthly budget constraint is

$$25q_{books} + 10q_{food} = 500.$$

Let's graph this budget constraint with books on the horizontal axis. Since the price of books is $25 per book, if Joe devoted all his allowance to buying books, he could buy $500/25 = 20$ books. Thus, the horizontal intercept is the point $(20, 0)$, which corresponds to a basket with only books and no food. Likewise, since the price per meal is $10, the maximum number of meals per month that Joe could buy is $500/10 = 50$. The vertical intercept is the point $(0, 50)$, which corresponds to a basket of all food and no books.

We get the budget line by connecting the two extreme points. The slope of the constraint is the negative of the ratio of relative prices $-\frac{p_{books}}{p_{food}} = -\frac{25}{10} = -2.5$. The set of baskets that lies below the budget line represents the affordable combinations of books and food that Joe can buy with his income. The baskets that lie on the line exhaust all his income. Figure 1.14 depicts Joe's budget constraint.

Suppose now, that Joe's monthly allowance decreases to $250. This change in income means that the budget line $(25q_{books} + 10q_{food} = 250)$ would shift inward in a parallel way. The maximum number of books that Joe can buy with this income is $250/25 = 10$ and the maximum number of meals is

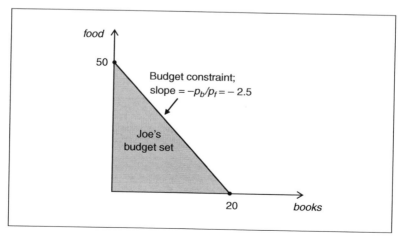

Figure 1.14 Example 1.2 Joe's Budget Constraint

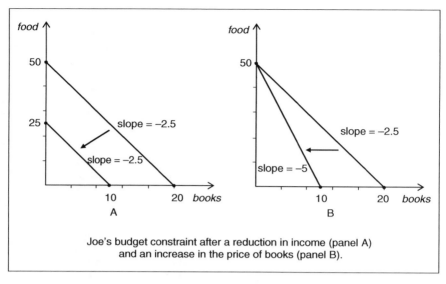

Joe's budget constraint after a reduction in income (panel A)
and an increase in the price of books (panel B).

Figure 1.15 Example 1.2 Changing Income and Prices

$250/10 = 25$. Thus, the horizontal intercept is the point $(10, 0)$ and the vertical intercept $(0, 25)$. The slope remains the same since the prices of the goods have not changed. Panel A of figure 1.15 depicts Joe's new budget constraint after the change in income.

Finally, let's analyze the effect of a change in the price of one of the goods. Assume that Joe's monthly income is again $500, but the price of books increases to $50 per book. Since the price of food is unchanged, if Joe spends all his income on food, he can still buy 50 meals at the most. Now, however, if he spends it all on books, the maximum number of books that he can buy is $500/50 = 10$. The budget constraint rotates inward due to the higher price of books. The slope of the budget line changes to $-\frac{p'_{books}}{p_{food}} = -\frac{50}{10} = -5$. Panel B of figure 1.15 depicts Joe's new budget constraint after the change in the price of books.

TEST YOUR UNDERSTANDING 3

(1) Mary must divide $120 between the consumption of good x and good z. Good x costs $15 per unit and good z costs $5 per unit.
   a. Graph Mary's budget constraint (with good x on the horizontal axis).
   b. Show what happens to the budget constraint if her income increases to $180.

(2) Alice has $400 to spend on good x and good z. The market prices for these goods are $p_x = \$10$ and $p_z = \$20$ per unit.

    a. Graph Alice's budget constraint (with good x on the horizontal axis).

    b. Show what happens to her budget constraint if the price of good z doubles.

(Solutions are in Appendix B)

1.5.4 Horizontal and Vertical Lines

We can also have linear equations of the form

$$y = a \text{ or } x = b,$$

where a and b are constants. The equation $y = a$ is the equation of a **horizontal line** with vertical intercept of $y = a$, no horizontal intercept, and slope equal to zero.

A **vertical line** is a special case since it is not a graph of a function.[6] The equation of a vertical line is given by $x = b$. The horizontal intercept of a vertical line is $x = b$, and there is no vertical intercept. The slope of a vertical line is undefined; the reason of this can be seen using the definition of slope: $\frac{\Delta y}{\Delta x}$. For a vertical line $\Delta x = 0$, and anything divided by zero is undefined. Figure 1.16 depicts both lines.

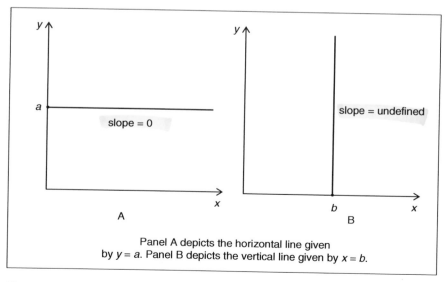

Panel A depicts the horizontal line given by $y = a$. Panel B depicts the vertical line given by $x = b$.

Figure 1.16   Horizontal and Vertical Lines

1.6 Solving Two-Variable Systems of Linear Equations

A two-variable **system of linear equations** is a set of two equations with two unknowns. The **solution** to this system of equations is the set of values of the unknowns that simultaneously satisfies both the equations. For a linear system of equations, this solution is typically a unique solution.[7]

One way to solve a system of two equations and two unknowns is as follows:[8]

STEP 1. Start with two equations like these:

$$y = 2 + x, \tag{1.6}$$

$$y = 14 - 2x. \tag{1.7}$$

STEP 2. Take the right-hand side of equation (1.6), that is, $2 + x$, and substitute it into the value of y wherever y appears in the equation (1.7). This leaves us with a single equation in terms of x:

$$2 + x = 14 - 2x. \tag{1.8}$$

STEP 3. Collect like terms by moving $-2x$ and 2 to the opposite sides of equation (1.8) to get:

$$x + 2x = 14 - 2.$$

Simplifying, we get $3x = 12$. Then, we divide both sides by 3, $\frac{3x}{3} = \frac{12}{3}$, and simplifying, we find that $x = \frac{12}{3} = 4$.

STEP 4. Plugging the result of $x = 4$ into equation (1.6), we get $y = 2+4 = 6$. Hence, the values $x^* = 4$ and $y^* = 6$ solve the original two equations.

This system is graphed in figure 1.17. In a system of two linear equations and two unknowns, the solution (x^*, y^*) represents the intersection of the two lines in a graph.

Progress Exercises

Find the values of x and y that simultaneously solve both equations in each of the following systems.

1. $y = 10 - x$
   $y = 5 + 4x.$

   Solution:
   $x^* = 1$ and $y^* = 9.$

2. $y = 30 - 2x$
   $y = x - 3.$

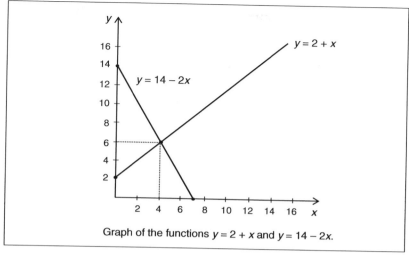

Graph of the functions $y = 2 + x$ and $y = 14 - 2x$.

Figure 1.17 Solving a System of Equations

Solution:
$x^* = 11$ and $y^* = 8$.

3. $y + x = 20$
$y = 4x$.

Solution:
$x^* = 4$ and $y^* = 16$.

4. $y + 3 = 2x$
$x + y = 3$.

Solution:
$x^* = 2$ and $y^* = 1$.

5. $2x = 2y - 6$
$x = 5 - y$.

Solution:
$x^* = 1$ and $y^* = 4$.

6. $\frac{1}{2}x + 2y = 4$
$10 - 2x = 6y$.

Solution:
$x^* = -4$ and $y^* = 3$.

Application 1.7 Market Equilibrium
If we add up the individual demand curves of all the consumers in the market, we get the *market demand*. Similarly, to get the *market supply*, we add

the individual supply curves of all the sellers in the market. In a *competitive market*, individual consumers and suppliers are *price-takers*, which means that their individual actions cannot affect the market price.

Suppose then, that the demand and supply functions in a certain market are given by

$$Q^d = 21 - p$$
$$Q^s = 2p,$$

where the *d* and *s* superscripts denote "demand" and "supply." A *market equilibrium* occurs at the point where the supply and demand functions intersect. At the *equilibrium price*, p^*, the amount that suppliers want to sell is equal to the amount that consumers want to buy. This amount is called the *equilibrium quantity*, Q^*.

The method of solving for the equilibrium price and quantity is as follows:

STEP 1. Set demand equal to supply $Q^d = Q^s$.

In our particular example, we obtain $21 - p = 2p$.

STEP 2. Now that you have an equation that only depends on p, solve for p to find the equilibrium price p^*.

In our case, we simply need to move the term $-p$ to the other side of the equation. This results in $21 = 2p + p$. Then, simplifying, we get $21 = 3p$. Finally, we divide both sides by 3, $\frac{3p}{3} = \frac{21}{3}$, and get the equilibrium price $p^* = 7$.

STEP 3. Substitute the equilibrium price p^* into either the demand or the supply functions to get the equilibrium quantity, Q^*.

In our example, if we substitute in the demand equation, we find out that $Q^* = 21 - 7 = 14$. This is the same result that we would have obtained using the supply equation instead, that is, $Q^* = 2(7) = 14$. Figure 1.18 shows the graph of both lines and illustrates that the point $(Q^*, p^*) = (14, 7)$ corresponds to the intersection of the demand and supply curves.

Example 1.3: Equilibrium in a particular market

The following demand and supply functions describe the market for natural gas in a particular region. The *g* subscript denotes "natural gas" and the *o* subscript denotes "oil." The *s* and *d* superscripts refer to "supply" and "demand," respectively.

$$Q_g^s = 16 + 2p_g,$$
$$Q_g^d = 3.75p_o - 5p_g.$$

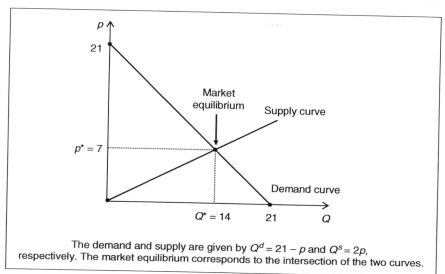

The demand and supply are given by $Q^d = 21 - p$ and $Q^s = 2p$, respectively. The market equilibrium corresponds to the intersection of the two curves.

Figure 1.18 Market Equilibrium

If the price of oil is $p_o = 8$, what is the equilibrium price and quantity of natural gas?

Solution:

With a price of $p_o = 8$, the demand and supply functions become

$$Q_g^s = 16 + 2p_g \text{ and } Q_g^d = 30 - 5p_g.$$

To solve for equilibrium price, we set $Q_g^s = Q_g^d$ that implies $16 + 2p_g = 30 - 5p_g$. Solving for p_g, we find that the equilibrium price is $p_g^* = 2$. Now, we substitute this value into either the supply or demand to arrive at the equilibrium quantity of $Q_g^* = 20$.

TEST YOUR UNDERSTANDING 4

(1) If the supply and demand functions in certain market are given by $Q^d = 26 - p$ and $Q^s = 5 + 2p$, find the equilibrium price and quantity.

(2) If the supply and demand functions in certain market are given by $Q^d = 25 - 2p$ and $Q^s = 3p$, find the equilibrium price and quantity.

(3) Suppose that in a fictitious town the demand for cartons of cigarettes is given by the equation $Q^d = 100,000$ while the supply of cartons of cigarettes is given by the equation $Q^s = 5,000p$. Find the equilibrium price and quantity in this market.

(*Solutions are in Appendix B*).

1.7 Properties of Functions

A function is **continuous** if it displays no "jumps" and no "holes." Intuitively, a continuous function is one that can be drawn without lifting the pencil from the paper. Examples of continuous and discontinuous functions are illustrated in figure 1.19.

A **smooth** function is one that has no "kinks" or corners. When there is a kink in the function, the slope of the function will be different before and after the kink. Figure 1.20 illustrates an example of a kink in a function.

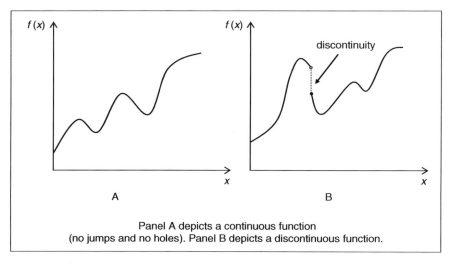

Panel A depicts a continuous function
(no jumps and no holes). Panel B depicts a discontinuous function.

Figure 1.19 Continuous and Discontinuous Functions

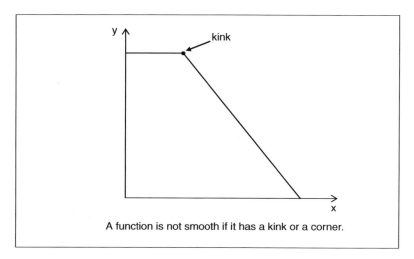

A function is not smooth if it has a kink or a corner.

Figure 1.20 Kinks in a Function

If the function $y = f(x)$ is both continuous and smooth, then it is **differentiable**, which means that the derivative of the function exists (derivatives are covered in chapter 2). Finally, a **monotonic** function is one that always increases or always decreases. Consequently, the slope of a monotonic function is always positive or always negative.

Application 1.8   Kinked Budget Constraints

In many economic decisions faced by consumers, the budget constraints might be nonlinear. A few of the more common examples are:

- *Quantity rationing constraints*: this means that the level of consumption of some good is fixed to be no larger than a certain amount.
- *Quantity discounts*: these may take the form, for example, of price reductions that affect the total number of units bought or of price reductions that apply only to the additional units bought beyond a certain threshold.

Suppose, for example, that a consumer faces the following simple quantity discount scheme: if more than x^m units of good x are bought, the consumer pays a lower price for all the additional units beyond this threshold. Since the slope of the budget constraint is the ratio of relative prices, if the price of good x for units less than x^m is different from the price for units more than x^m, the slope of these two segments will also be different. The budget constraint will have a kink precisely at the threshold quantity, x^m. Figure 1.21 depicts the consumer's budget constraint in this case.

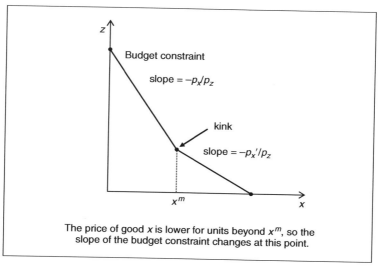

Figure 1.21   Budget Constraint with Quantity Discounts

Example 1.4: Quantity discounts

Suppose that a consumer has an income of $1,000 and that she consumes two goods, good x and good z. The price per unit of good z is $p_z = \$10$. The price of good x depends on how much is purchased. For up to 20 units, the price per unit of good x is $p_x = \$20$. From the 21st unit onward, the price per unit goes down to $p_{x_d} = \$10$. Draw the consumer's budget constraint.

Solution:

We know that if the consumer devotes all her income to good z, she would be able to buy $1000/10 = 100$ units of good z. So, the starting point of the budget constraint on the vertical axis is the point $(0, 100)$.

Now, if she devotes all her income to good x, she would be able to buy the first 20 units at a price of $20, which implies an expenditure of $400. The 21st unit onward cost $10, so, with her remaining $600, she would be able to buy $600/10 = 60$ units of good x. In this case, she would have a total of 80 units of good x, which corresponds to the point $(80, 0)$.

What is left is to indicate the different slopes of the budget constraint. The slope is $-\frac{p_x}{p_z} = -\frac{20}{10} = -2$ for units of good x lower than 20 and from the 21st unit onward, the slope changes to $-\frac{p_{x_d}}{p_z} = -\frac{10}{10} = -1$. Figure 1.22 shows this budget constraint.

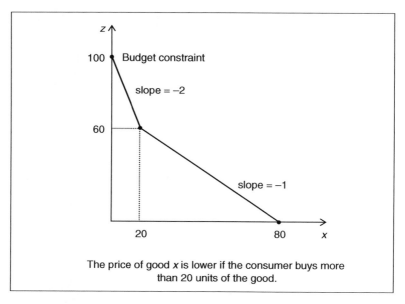

Figure 1.22 Example 1.4. Quantity Discounts

1.8 Exponents

Powers of numbers or variables can be expressed by using superscripts called **exponents**. In the expression x^n, read as "x to the nth power," x is referred to as the **base** and n is the **exponent**. The function $f(x) = x^n$, where n is a real number is called a **power function**.

In general, for $x \neq 0$, the following basic rules apply (x is for exponent):

RULE 1x. $x^0 = 1$.
RULE 2x. $x^a \times x^b = x^{a+b}$.
RULE 3x. $(x^a)^b = x^{ab}$.
RULE 4x. $(xz)^a = x^a \times z^a$.
RULE 5x. $\left(\frac{x}{z}\right)^a = \frac{x^a}{z^a}$.
RULE 6x. $\frac{x^a}{x^b} = x^{a-b}$.
RULE 7x. $x^{-a} = \frac{1}{x^a}$ and $\frac{1}{x^{-a}} = x^a$.

Finally, if the variable is raised to the first power, that is x^1, the exponent is not written. It is understood that x is raised to the power 1.

Examples:

Simplify the following expressions:

1. $x^3 \times x^2$

   Solution: x^5

2. $(x^2)^5$

   Solution: x^{10}

3. $\frac{x^8}{x^2}$

   Solution: x^6

Application 1.9   Cobb–Douglas Production Function
A production function measures the maximum amount of output that a firm can get from a given amount of input. Suppose that output q is produced using two inputs: labor L and capital K. The production function is a *Cobb–Douglas production function* if it has the form:

$$q(L, K) = AL^a K^b.$$

The parameter A measures the overall effectiveness with which capital and labor are used. The parameters a and b measure how output responds to changes in the amount of L and K, respectively.

1.8.1 Radicals and Fractional Exponents

A **radical** is an indicated root of a number or variable such as $\sqrt{20}$, $\sqrt{x}$, or $\sqrt[3]{5x}$. The symbol $\sqrt{}$ is called a **radical sign**.

In the expression $\sqrt[a]{x}$, the number represented by a is called the **index**. The index indicates which root is to be taken. In square roots, the index 2 is not written.

A positive number has two square roots that have opposite signs. For example, the square roots of 9 are ± 3. The **principal square root** of a number is its *positive* square root. The radical sign is used to indicate the principal square root. Thus, $\sqrt{9}$ = principal square root of 9 = 3. A negative sign is placed before the radical sign to indicate the negative square root, for example, $-\sqrt{9} = -3$.

The following rules apply for square roots (r is for root):

RULE 1r. $\sqrt{x} \cdot \sqrt{z} = \sqrt{xz}$.

RULE 2r. $\frac{\sqrt{x}}{\sqrt{z}} = \sqrt{\frac{x}{z}}$.

RULE 3r. $\sqrt{0} = 0$.

RULE 4r. $\sqrt{x} \geq 0$.

RULE 5r. $\sqrt{x^3} = x \cdot \sqrt{x} \geq 0$.

A **fractional exponent** is defined as:

$$x^{\frac{n}{a}} = \left(\sqrt[a]{x}\right)^n = \sqrt[a]{x^n},$$

where if a is even, then x must be nonnegative. The fractional exponent $1/2$ (or 0.5) indicates square root.

Example 1.5: The production function in a particular firm
Consider a firm that uses workers, L, and machines, K, to produce output q according to the following Cobb-Douglas production function:

$$q = 10L^{0.5}K^{0.5}.$$

Suppose that the relation between capital and labor for this particular firm should be $K = \frac{L}{4}$ (i.e., 4 workers for every machine). How many workers and machines are required to meet a production target of 140 units?

Solution:
First, substitute the information given in the production function:

$$140 = 10L^{0.5}\left(\frac{L}{4}\right)^{0.5}.$$

Then, we can apply our rules to simplify as follows:

$$140 = 10\frac{\sqrt{L} \cdot \sqrt{L}}{\sqrt{4}} \quad \text{(Following R\textsc{ule} 2r)},$$

$$140 = 10\frac{L}{2} \quad \text{(Following R\textsc{ule} 2x)}.$$

Solving for L results in $L^* = 28$. Finally, to find K^*, substitute into the relation given to us:

$$K^* = \frac{L}{4} = \frac{28}{4} = 7.$$

So, the input mix required to produce 140 units is 28 workers and 7 machines.

1.8.2 *Homogenous Functions**

A function $f(x, z)$ is called **homogenous of degree k** if for every $t > 0$, we have

$$f(tx, tz) = t^k f(x, z).$$

A case worthy of note is when a function is **homogenous of degree 1** (or linearly homogenous). In this case, a proportionate increase in *all* the variables (i.e., x and z) leads to the same proportionate increase in the value of the function. For example, doubling all variables doubles the value of the function, tripling all the variables triples the value of the function, and so on.

Application 1.10   Constant Returns to Scale
Suppose that we have the following Cobb-Douglas production function:

$$q(L, K) = AL^a K^{1-a}. \tag{1.9}$$

Note that the exponents of L and K in equation (1.9) were chosen so that their sum is equal to one. This function is homogenous of degree 1. We can verify it by multiplying both variables, L and K, by the same factor t. We find that

$$q(tL, tK) = A(tL)^a (tK)^{1-a}$$

$$= At^a L^a t^{1-a} K^{1-a} \quad \text{(Following R\textsc{ule} 4x)}$$

$$= tAL^a K^{1-a} \quad \text{(Following R\textsc{ule} 2x)}$$

$$= tq(L, K).$$

The economic interpretation of this property is that a proportionate increase in both inputs, L and K, leads to the same proportionate increase in output q. If, for example, L and K are doubled, then q doubles as well. Economists refer to such a production function as one that exhibits *constant returns to scale*.

1.9 CHANGES AND GROWTH RATES

Suppose that the value of the variable x changes over time. If x_1 denotes the variable's initial value and x_2 its final value, then the change in x is given by $\Delta x = x_2 - x_1$.

To get the **change rate** (or **percent change**) of x, we simply need to divide the change in x, Δx, by the variable's initial value and then multiply this by 100 (so that we get the answer in percentage points). Let $\%\Delta x$ denote the percent change of x, then we have that

$$\%\Delta x = \frac{x_2 - x_1}{x_1} \times 100.$$

Examples:

Calculate the percent change in x if x_1 denotes the variable's initial value and x_2 its final value.

1. $x_1 = 10$ and $x_2 = 13$
   Solution: $\%\Delta x = 30\%$.

2. $x_1 = 50$ and $x_2 = 45$
   Solution: $\%\Delta x = -10\%$.

3. $x_1 = 1.2$ and $x_2 = 1.8$
   Solution: $\%\Delta x = 50\%$.

Example 1.6: Economic growth
Table 1.2 reports the values of the capital input, K, and labor input, L, in two different years for a particular economy. By how much did capital and labor grow from year 1 to year 2?

Solution:
Using the change rate formula, we find that $\%\Delta K = \frac{2,520-2,400}{2,400} \times 100 = 5\%$ and $\%\Delta L = \frac{86.9-79}{79} \times 100 = 10\%$.

Table 1.2 Capital and Labor

Year	K (billions of dollars)	L (millions of workers)
1	2,400	79.0
2	2,520	86.9

1.9.1 Growth Rate Formulas

Let x and z be any two variables, not necessarily related by a function, that are changing over time. Let $\%\Delta x$ and $\%\Delta z$ represent the percent growth of x and z, respectively. The following rules provide useful approximations when calculating growth rates (g stands for growth):

RULE 1g. The percent growth rate of the product of x and z is approximately equal to the percent growth rate of x plus the percent growth rate of z. That is,

$$\text{\% growth rate of } (xz) = \%\Delta x + \%\Delta z.$$

RULE 2g. The percent growth rate of the ratio of x to z is approximately equal to the percent growth rate of x minus the percent growth rate of z. That is,

$$\text{\% growth rate of } \left(\frac{x}{z}\right) = \%\Delta x - \%\Delta z.$$

RULE 3g. The percent growth rate of x raised to the power a (where a is a constant) is approximately equal to a times the percent growth rate of x. That is,

$$\text{\% growth rate of } (x^a) = a(\%\Delta x).$$

Examples:

Let x_1 denote the initial value of the variable x and x_2 its final value. Let z_1 denote the initial value of the variable z and z_2 its final value.

$x_1 = 10$ and $x_2 = 13$

$z_1 = 5$ and $z_2 = 7$.

1. Calculate the percent growth rate of the product of x and z.
   Solution:
   $\text{\% growth rate of } (xz) = \%\Delta x + \%\Delta z = 30\% + 40\% = 70\%.$

2. Calculate the percent growth rate of the ratio of x to z.
   Solution:
   $\text{\% growth rate of } \left(\frac{x}{z}\right) = \%\Delta x - \%\Delta z = 30\% - 40\% = -10\%.$

3. Calculate the percent growth rate of x^2.
   Solution:
   $\text{\% growth rate of } (x^2) = 2(\%\Delta x) = 2(30\%) = 60\%.$

4. Calculate the percent growth rate of $z^{0.5}$.
   Solution:

% growth rate of $(z^{0.5}) = 0.5(\%\Delta z) = 0.5(40\%) = 20\%$.

Application 1.11 The Sources of Economic Growth
The amount of output that an economy produces depends on two factors:
(1) the quantities of inputs (such as labor and capital) utilized in the production process, and (2) the productivity of the inputs. The effectiveness
with which capital and labor are used is summarized by a relation called the
aggregate production function. Empirical studies show that the aggregate production function of the U.S. economy is described reasonably well by the
following Cobb-Douglas production function:

$$Y = AK^{0.3}L^{0.7}, \tag{1.10}$$

where
  Y = total output produced in a given period of time;
  A = measure of the overall capital and labor productivity;
  K = capital stock or quantity of capital used in the period; and
  L = number of workers employed in the period.

For an economy such as that described in equation (1.10), there are three
key determinants of economic growth: accumulation of capital (increases
in K), population growth (increases in L), and productivity improvements
(increases in A). In particular, the relationship between the growth rate of output, $\%\Delta Y$, and the growth rate of inputs, $\%\Delta K$ and $\%\Delta L$, and productivity,
$\%\Delta A$, is given by:

$$\%\Delta Y = \%\Delta A + 0.3(\%\Delta K) + 0.7(\%\Delta L). \tag{1.11}$$

Equation (1.11) is called the *growth accounting equation*, and it is simply the
production function written in (percent) growth rate form.

Example 1.6: Economic growth (continued)
Assume that this economy's aggregate production function is given by:

$$Y = 10K^{0.3}L^{0.7}.$$

By how much did output grow from year 1 to year 2?
Solution:
We had already calculated the growth rate of capital and labor, 5% and 10%,
respectively. Now, to get the growth rate of output, we need to substitute
these results into the growth accounting equation as follows:

$$\%\Delta Y = 0.3(5) + 0.7(10) = 8.5\%.$$

1.9.2   Index Numbers*

An **index number** is a relative number that describes data that are changing over time. Index numbers are used to relate a variable in one period of time to the same variable in another period called the *base period*.

Suppose that we are analyzing how variable x changes over time. Assume that we have data on the values of x for n periods of time. That is, we have a data set that consists of observations x_t from period $t = 0$ to period $t = n$.

We can choose any period from $t = 0, \ldots, n$ as the base period. Denote the chosen base period by t_{base} and the value of x in such period by $x_{t_{base}}$; the index numbers for $t = 0, \ldots, n$ are obtained as follows:

$$Index_t = \frac{x_t}{x_{t_{base}}} \times 100.$$

It is conventional to multiply by 100 to obtain an index number that takes the value of 100 for the base period.

Index numbers simplify the comparison of values of x over time. For example, an index of 110 means that there has been a 10% increase in the value of x since the base period. Similarly, an index of 90 means that there has been a 10% decrease in the value of x since the base period.

Application 1.12   Consumer Price Index and Inflation

A *price index* is a measure of the average level of prices for some specified set of goods and services, relative to the prices in a base year. The most commonly used measure of the level of prices is the *Consumer Price Index* (CPI). The CPI measures the prices paid by urban consumers for a market basket of consumer goods and services.

Each month, data collectors from the Bureau of Labor Statistics find out the current prices of the goods and services in a fixed market basket.[9] Currently, the reference base period is 1982–1984, which means that the CPI is constructed so that it averages 100 for this three-year period. So, if the CPI is 177 in 2008, this means that the average level of consumer prices is 77% higher in 2008 than it was in the 1982–1984 period.

Since the CPI measures the level of prices, one way we can estimate *inflation* is by computing the change in the CPI from one period to another. That is, if CPI_t is the price level in period t and CPI_{t+1} is the price level in period $t + 1$, the inflation rate denoted by π (pi), between t and $t + 1$, is

$$\pi_{t+1} = \frac{CPI_{t+1} - CPI_t}{CPI_t}.$$

Example 1.7: Calculation of a simple CPI index

To illustrate the construction of the CPI index, let's consider a simple case in which a consumer, Mary, buys 5 apples and 2 books every period.

In the base period, let's call it period 1, the prices of the goods are $0.50 per apple and $10 per book. Since period 1 is the base period, the CPI for this period is $CPI_1 = 100$. Now, suppose that the following period, period 2, the price of apples rises to $1 and the price of books remains unchanged. Let's calculate the CPI for period 2

$$CPI_2 = \frac{(5 \times \text{price of apples in period 2}) + (2 \times \text{price of books in period 2})}{(5 \times \text{price of apples in base period}) + (2 \times \text{price of books in base period})} \times 100$$

$$= \frac{(5 \times 1) + (2 \times 10)}{(5 \times 0.5) + (2 \times 10)} \times 100$$

$$= 111.11.$$

This index tells us how much it costs in the period 2 to buy a basket of 5 apples and 2 books relative to how much it costs to buy the same basket of goods in period 1 (base period). We can now calculate the inflation rate between period 1 and period 2

$$\pi_2 = \frac{CPI_2 - CPI_1}{CPI_1} = \frac{111.11 - 100}{100} = 0.1111.$$

The inflation rate between the two periods is 11.11%.

PRACTICE EXERCISES

1. Solve the equation $2y - 14 = 10 - 2x$ for y in terms of x.
2. Solve the equation $5 + 3x + y - 16 = 4 - 2y - 6x - 6$ for y in terms of x.
3. Solve the equation $\frac{y}{2} - 10 = x + 5$ for y in terms of x.
4. Find the value of x that solves the equation $3x - 15 = 10 - 2x$.
5. Find the value of x that solves the equation $x - 2x + 5 = 3x - 19$.
6. Graph the line $y = 10 - 2x$ with the variable x on the horizontal axis. Indicate the slope and the intercepts with the axes (depict only the first quadrant of the Cartesian plane).
7. Graph the line $x + 2y = 2$ with the variable x on the horizontal axis. Indicate the slope and the intercepts with the axes (depict only the first quadrant of the Cartesian plane).

8. Graph the function $16 - x = 2y$ with the variable x on the horizontal axis. Indicate the slope of the line and the intercepts with the axes (depict only the first quadrant of the Cartesian plane).

9. Graph the line $y = 10$ and the line $x = 5$ with the variable x on the horizontal axis. Indicate the slope and the intercepts with the axes of each line (depict only the first quadrant of the Cartesian plane).

10. Solve the equation $3x - y - 2 = 10 - 3y + x$ for y as a function of x and graph the line with the variable x on the horizontal axis. The variables y and x can only assume nonnegative values. Indicate the slope and the intercepts with the axes.

11. You are given the following system of equations:

$$y = 30 - x$$
$$y = 5 + 4x.$$

Find the values of x and y that simultaneously solve both equations.

12. You are given the following system of equations:

$$y + x = 10$$
$$y = 2 + x.$$

Find the values of x and y that simultaneously solve both equations.

13. You are given the following system of equations:

$$y = 3 - x$$
$$x = 2y.$$

Find the values of x and y that simultaneously solve both equations.

14. You are given the following system of equations:

$$y + x = 30$$
$$x = 10.$$

Find the values of x and y that simultaneously solve both equations. Graph both functions with the variable x on the horizontal axis. The variables y and x can only assume nonnegative values. Indicate the slope of each line and all intercepts with the axes.

15. You are given the following system of equations:

$$p = 12 - Q$$
$$p = \frac{1}{2}Q.$$

Find the values of Q and p that simultaneously solve both equations. Graph both functions with the variable p on the vertical axis. The variables Q and p can only assume nonnegative values. Indicate the slope of each line and all intercepts with the axes.

16. A consumer has income of $200. Good x costs $4 per unit and good y costs $10 per unit.
    (a) Graph the consumer's budget constraint with good x on the horizontal axis.
    (b) Show what happens to the budget constraint if the price of good y falls to $5.

17. A consumer has income of $500. Good x costs $10 per unit and good y costs $25 per unit.
    (a) Graph the consumer's budget constraint with good x on the horizontal axis.
    (b) Show what happens to the budget constraint if her income decreases to $250.

18. A consumer has income of $300. Good x costs $10 per unit and good y costs $20 per unit.
    (a) Graph the consumer's budget constraint with good x on the horizontal axis.
    (b) Show what happens to the budget constraint if the price of good x increases to $15 per unit and the price of good y decreases to $15 per unit.

19. If the supply and demand functions in a certain market are given by $Q^d = 30 - 2p$ and $Q^s = 4p$. Find the equilibrium price and quantity (remember that at equilibrium, demand and supply are equal).

20. If the supply and demand functions in a certain market are given by $Q^d = 20 - p$ and $Q^s = 5 + 2p$. Find the equilibrium price and quantity (remember that at equilibrium, demand and supply are equal).

21. Suppose that demand for beer is given by

$$Q^d_{beer} = 120 - 4p_{beer} + 3p_{wine} + 2I,$$

and supply is given by

$$Q^s_{beer} = 100 + 6p_{beer}.$$

Suppose that $p_{wine} = 20$ and $I = 10$. What is the equilibrium price and quantity of beer?

22. Peter is an avid movie watcher. He has budgeted $80 per month to watching movies at home (videos) and at the movie theater. The price of movie tickets is $8 per ticket and the price of rentals is $2 per video. Draw Peter's budget constraint (with videos on the x-axis). Indicate the slope of the line.

23. The following demand and supply functions describe the market for beef. The b subscript denotes "beef," the c subscript denotes "chicken," and the f subscript denotes "fish." The s and d superscripts denote "supply" and "demand," respectively.

$$Q_b^s = 20 + 2p_b,$$
$$Q_b^d = 4p_f + 7p_c - 10p_b.$$

What is the equilibrium price of beef when $p_f = 10$ and $p_c = 4$? What is the equilibrium quantity of beef traded?

24. Assume that the economy's aggregate production function is the following:

$$Y = 10K^{0.3}L^{0.7}.$$

In a particular year, the capital stock grows by 2% and the number of workers grows by 3%. By how much does output grow?

25. Assume that the economy's aggregate production function is the following:

$$Y = 10K^{0.3}L^{0.7}.$$

In a particular year, the capital stock grows by 2% and output grows by 3.4%. What can you say about the growth rate of labor?

CHAPTER 2

Business Math: Optimization

In most business applications, we seek to make the best use of the resources available. For example, a manager might need to decide how to allocate an advertising budget to maximize sales of a new product or might need to decide how much inventory to keep to minimize costs. Optimization is the analytical tool used when a decision maker seeks to make the best (optimal) choice, taking into account any possible limitations or restrictions on the choices.

2.1 NONLINEAR FUNCTIONS

A function $y = f(x)$ is a linear function if it has the form $y = a + bx$. As we discussed in chapter 1, the graph of a linear function is a straight line and its slope is constant. Now, we will introduce a different type of function, nonlinear functions. These functions will have important applications, particularly in optimization problems that deal with finding a maximum value (e.g., maximum profit) or a minimum value (e.g., minimum cost).

A function $y = f(x)$ is a **nonlinear function** if it cannot be expressed in the form $y = a + bx$. A nonlinear function has the property that its slope changes as the value of x changes. We will discuss how to calculate slopes of nonlinear functions below. For now, let's introduce the concepts of *concavity* and *convexity*.

The function $f(x)$ is **concave** if for every pair of points on its graph, the chord (or secant line) joining these two points lies below the graph. The function $f(x)$ is **convex** if for every pair of points on its graph, the chord joining them lies above the graph. Figure 2.1 illustrates both types of functions.

2.2 THE CONCEPT OF A DERIVATIVE

Suppose that y is a function of x given by $y = f(x)$. As you may recall, the slope of the function is given by

$$slope = \frac{\Delta y}{\Delta x}.$$

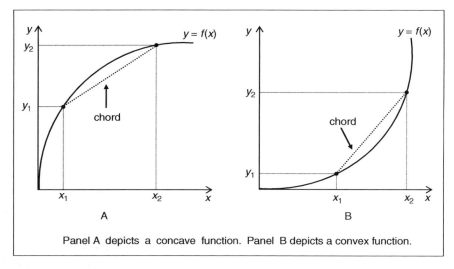

Panel A depicts a concave function. Panel B depicts a convex function.

Figure 2.1 Concave and Convex Functions

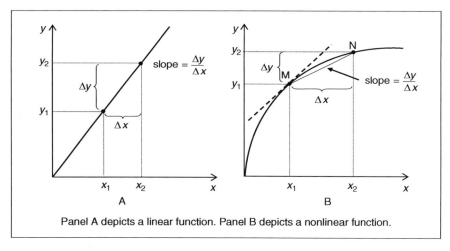

Panel A depicts a linear function. Panel B depicts a nonlinear function.

Figure 2.2 Linear and Nonlinear Functions

Now, consider the functions depicted in figure 2.2. For a linear function, such as the one in panel A, the magnitude of the change in x, Δx, and the change in y, Δy, has no impact on the value of the slope. The reason for this is that the slope of a linear function is constant.

This is not the case, however, for nonlinear functions. With a nonlinear function like that in panel B, the slope varies along the function. As a result, the magnitude of Δx and Δy affects the value of the slope. If we were to use the formula $\Delta y / \Delta x$ to calculate the slope of the function between points

(x_1, y_1) and (x_2, y_2), what we would get is the slope of the line segment that connects points M and N. This is not the same as the slope of the function at either point M or point N. However, if we make Δx smaller and smaller, then the slope will approximate the value of the slope of a line drawn *tangent* to the function at point M. The precise mathematical measure to evaluate the slope of a function when Δx is an infinitesimally small value is the **derivative**.

We will expand on the graphical interpretation of the derivative. Let's first review the notation and some useful rules for calculating derivatives.

2.2.1 Notation of Derivatives

The derivative of the function $y = f(x)$ with respect to x is typically denoted by $f'(x)$ and is read "f prime of x." This is the notation that we will use throughout; however, there are other ways to denote derivatives. Another common notation of derivatives requires the use of new symbols. The symbol for a "small (infinitesimal) change in the variable x" is dx (this does not mean d times x). We denote the derivative of $y = f(x)$ with respect to x as: $\frac{dy}{dx}$. Note that $\frac{dy}{dx}$ is not a fraction, it is a single symbol for the derivative. This notation reinforces the idea that the derivate is a rate of change. It indicates that the derivative of y with respect to x gives us the change in y that results from an infinitesimal change in x.

2.2.2 Rules of Differentiation

When we find the derivative of a function, we *differentiate* the function. Here are the basic rules of differentiation (d is for derivative).

RULE 1d. If $f(x) = c$, where c is a constant, then $f'(x) = 0$.

A derivative indicates a rate of change and, by definition, a constant never changes, so the derivative of a constant is always zero.

Examples:

1. If $f(x) = 3$, find $f'(x)$.
   Solution: $f'(x) = 0$.

2. If $f(x) = 16^2$, find $f'(x)$.
   Solution: $f'(x) = 0$.

3. If $f(x) = \sqrt{525}$, find $f'(x)$.
   Solution: $f'(x) = 0$.

RULE 2d. If $f(x) = x^a$, where a is any number, then $f'(x) = ax^{a-1}$.

The first step is to multiply x by the exponent a, that is, bring a down to multiply x. Then, subtract 1 from the exponent so that x is now raised to the power of $a - 1$.

Examples:

1. If $f(x) = x^3$, find $f'(x)$.

   Solution: $f'(x) = 3x^{3-1} = 3x^2$.

2. If $f(x) = x$, find $f'(x)$.

   Solution:
   $f'(x) = 1x^{1-1} = 1x^0 = 1$. Remember that any number raised to the power zero is 1.

3. If $f(x) = \sqrt{x}$, find $f'(x)$.

   Solution:
   $f'(x) = \frac{1}{2}x^{\frac{1}{2}-1} = \frac{1}{2}x^{-\frac{1}{2}} = \frac{1}{2} \cdot \frac{1}{\sqrt{x}}$. Remember that the fractional exponent $1/2$ indicates square root.

RULE 3d. If $f(x) = cg(x)$, where c is a constant, then $f'(x) = cg'(x)$.

In this case, c is multiplying $g(x)$, which is a function of x, so the constant c will continue to multiply the derivative $g'(x)$. The derivative of $g(x)$ is taken according to RULE 2d.

Examples:

1. If $f(x) = 4x^3$, find $f'(x)$.

   Solution: $f'(x) = 4\left(3x^2\right) = 12x^2$.

2. If $f(x) = -5x^2$, find $f'(x)$.

   Solution: $f'(x) = -5\left(2x^1\right) = -10x$.

3. If $f(x) = 8x^4$, find $f'(x)$.

   Solution: $f'(x) = 8(4x^3) = 32x^3$.

RULE 4d. If $f(x) = g(x) + h(x)$, then $f'(x) = g'(x) + h'(x)$ and if $f(x) = g(x) - h(x)$, then $f'(x) = g'(x) - h'(x)$.

The derivative of the sum (difference) of two or more functions equals the sum (difference) of their respective derivatives.

Examples:

1. If $g(x) = 4x$, $h(x) = x^2$ and $f(x) = g(x) + h(x)$, find $f'(x)$.

   Solution: $f'(x) = g'(x) + h'(x) = 4 + 2x$.

2. If $g(x) = 12x$, $h(x) = 2x^4$ and $f(x) = g(x) - h(x)$, find $f'(x)$.

   Solution: $f'(x) = g'(x) - h'(x) = 12 - 8x^3$.

3. If $g(x) = x^3 + 5$, $h(x) = 20x$ and $f(x) = g(x) - h(x)$, find $f'(x)$.

   Solution: $f'(x) = g'(x) - h'(x) = 3x^2 - 20$.

RULE 5d. If $f(x) = a + bx$, then $f'(x) = b$. (Follows from RULE 1d and RULE 2d). Note that this is the equation of a line and b is its slope.

Examples:

1. If $f(x) = 4x + 3$, find $f'(x)$.

   Solution: $f'(x) = 4$.

2. If $f(x) = 500 - 100x$, find $f'(x)$.

   Solution: $f'(x) = -100$.

3. If $f(x) = 4 - 3x$, find $f'(x)$.

   Solution: $f'(x) = -3$.

Application 2.1   Marginal Functions

In economics, it is conventional to refer to the derivative of a total function as a *marginal function*. For example, a firm's total cost function expresses the firm's costs in terms of the level of output. The firm's marginal cost measures the change in the firm's total cost due to a "small change" in its level of output.

To understand the concept of marginal functions better, consider first the following simple example in which a "small change" in output means a one-unit change. A firm produces output q at a total cost of $C(q)$. Table 2.1 shows the total costs for the firm at different levels of output. The marginal cost, denoted by MC, tells us how much costs go up following a *one-unit* increase in output.

Suppose that we know that the cost function of this firm is given by

$C(q) = 4q$.

Table 2.1   Calculating Marginal Cost

Quantity (Units)	Total Cost (Dollars)	Marginal Cost (Dollars)
1	4	$4 - 0 = 4$
2	8	$8 - 4 = 4$
3	12	$12 - 8 = 4$
4	16	$16 - 12 = 4$
5	20	$20 - 16 = 4$

We can now get the same marginal costs of table 2.1 by taking the derivative of the cost function. That is,

$$MC(q) = C'(q) = 4.$$

This means that for this particular firm, the cost of producing each additional unit is $4.

TEST YOUR UNDERSTANDING 1

(1) Suppose that a firm has a cost of production given by $C(q) = 5q + 2$. Find the firm's marginal cost (i.e., the derivative of the cost function).
(2) Suppose that a firm has a cost of production given by $C(q) = 2q^2 + 200$. Find the firm's marginal cost.

(*Solutions are in Appendix B*)

2.3 GRAPHICAL INTERPRETATION OF DERIVATIVES

As we mentioned earlier, the slope of a nonlinear function $f(x)$ at any point can be approximated by the slope of the line *tangent* to the function at that point. We can find the actual value of the slope using derivatives. Graphically, the derivative of a function evaluated at a given point is the slope of a line tangent to the curve at that point. That is, $f'(a)$ is the slope of the line tangent to the function at the point where $x = a$.

For example, suppose that we want to find the slope of the function $f(x) = x^2$ at the particular point where $x = 1$. First, we find the derivative of the function

$$f'(x) = 2x.$$

Then, we evaluate it at the specific point where $x = 1$,

$$f'(1) = 2 \cdot 1 = 2.$$

Since the slope of the line tangent to the function at point $(1, 1)$ is 2, we know that the slope of the function at that particular point is also 2. Figure 2.3 illustrates this graphically.

Notice that since the derivative gives us the slope of the function, we can interpret the sign of the derivative as the rate at which the function is changing. In general:

- If $f'(x) > 0$ on an interval (a, b), then $f(x)$ is increasing over that interval.
- If $f'(x) < 0$ on an interval (a, b), then $f(x)$ is decreasing over that interval.

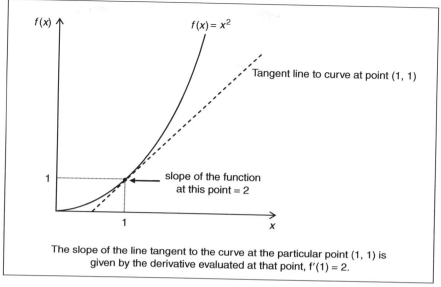

Figure 2.3   Graphical Interpretation of the Derivative

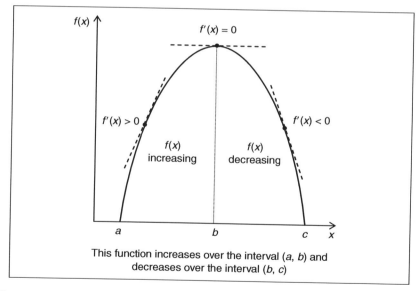

Figure 2.4   Increasing and Decreasing Functions

Figure 2.4 summarizes our discussion with an example. We will expand on these concepts when we talk about optimization.

Now, we should make a brief remark on the existence of the derivative. The function $y = f(x)$ is **differentiable** if its derivative exists. For the function

$y = f(x)$ to be differentiable at a point $x = x_0$, the function must be *continuous* (i.e., there are no gaps or breaks) and it must be *smooth* (i.e., there are no sharp points) at $x = x_0$.[1]

Progress Exercises

1. Consider the function $f(x) = 2x^2 + 6$. Find the slope of the line tangent to the function at the point where $x = 2$.

   Solution:
   First, we find the derivative of the function

   $$f'(x) = 4x.$$

   Then, we evaluate it at the specific point where $x = 2$,

   $$f'(2) = 4 \cdot 2 = 8.$$

   So, the slope of the line tangent to the function at $x = 2$ is 8.

2. Consider the function $f(x) = \sqrt{x} - 2$. Find the slope of the line tangent to the function at the point where $x = 4$.

   Solution:
   First, we find the derivative of the function

   $$f'(x) = \frac{1}{2}x^{-\frac{1}{2}} = \frac{1}{2} \cdot \frac{1}{\sqrt{x}}.$$

   Then, we evaluate it at $x = 4$,

   $$f'(4) = \frac{1}{2} \cdot \frac{1}{\sqrt{4}} = \frac{1}{2} \cdot \frac{1}{2} = \frac{1}{4}.$$

   So, the slope of the line tangent to the function at $x = 4$ is $\frac{1}{4}$.

Application 2.2   Marginal Product of Labor
Suppose that a firm produces output q using only one input: labor. Assume, in particular, that the firm has a production function given by

$$q = f(L) = 20L^{0.5}, \tag{2.1}$$

where L denotes number of workers. Figure 2.5 depicts the graph of the production function described in equation (2.1).

   Suppose that the firm currently employs 25 workers and produces $q(25) = 20(25)^{0.5} = 100$ units of output. How would the firm's output change if an additional worker is hired? The answer to this question lies in the concept of marginal product of labor.

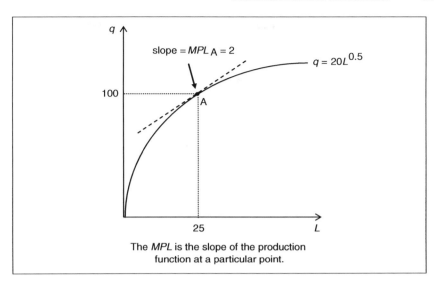

Figure 2.5 Marginal Product of Labor

The *marginal product of labor* (*MPL*) is defined as the increase in output that results from a one-unit increase in labor. Mathematically, *MPL* is the slope of the production function at a particular point.

Let's calculate the firm's *MPL* with the current 25 workers (i.e., the slope of the function at point A in figure 2.5). To calculate this slope, we first take the derivative of the production function, that is,

$$MPL_A = q'(L) = 20(0.5)L^{-0.5} = \frac{10}{\sqrt{L}}.$$

Then, we evaluate this derivative at the point $L = 25$ to get the specific value of the slope:

$$MPL_A = q'(25) = \frac{10}{\sqrt{25}} = \frac{10}{5} = 2.$$

This means that, with the existing labor force, hiring an additional worker (i.e., an additional unit of labor) would increase the firm's output by 2 units.

TEST YOUR UNDERSTANDING 2

Suppose that a firm has a production function given by $q = 12L^{0.5}$, where L denotes the number of workers in the firm.

a) How many units of output can be produced if the firm currently employs 4 workers?

b) What is the *MPL* at $L = 4$ (i.e., the slope of the function at this particular point)?

c) With the existing labor force, by how much would the firm's output change if the firm decided to hire an additional worker?

(*Solutions are in Appendix B*)

2.4 ADDITIONAL TOPICS ON DERIVATIVES*

The following rules enable us to calculate the derivative of a product of two functions, the derivative of a quotient of two functions, and the derivative of a function raised to some power n.

PRODUCT RULE. If $f(x) = g(x) \cdot h(x)$, then $f'(x) = [g(x) \cdot h'(x)] + [h(x) \cdot g'(x)]$.

The derivative of a product of two functions is the first function times the derivative of the second function plus the second function times the derivative of the first function.

Examples:

1. If $g(x) = x^2$, $h(x) = 4x + 2$, and $f(x) = g(x) \cdot h(x)$, find $f'(x)$.

   Solution:
   $$f'(x) = [x^2 (4)] + [(4x + 2) 2x] = 4x^2 + 8x^2 + 4x = 12x^2 + 4x.$$

2. If $g(x) = 3x$, $h(x) = 1 - x^2$, and $f(x) = g(x) \cdot h(x)$, find $f'(x)$.

   Solution:
   $$f'(x) = [3x (-2x)] + [(1 - x^2) 3] = -6x^2 + 3 - 3x^2 = 3 - 9x^2.$$

3. If $g(x) = x$, $h(x) = x^3 + 15$, and $f(x) = g(x) \cdot h(x)$, find $f'(x)$.

   Solution:
   $$f'(x) = [x (3x^2)] + [(x^3 + 15) 1] = 3x^3 + x^3 + 15 = 4x^3 + 15.$$

QUOTIENT RULE. If $f(x) = \frac{g(x)}{h(x)}$, then $f'(x) = \frac{[h(x) \cdot g'(x)] - [g(x) \cdot h'(x)]}{[h(x)]^2}$.

The derivative of a quotient of two functions is the denominator times the derivative of the numerator minus the numerator times the derivative of the denominator, all over the denominator squared.

Examples:

1. If $g(x) = x + 1$, $h(x) = x^2$, and $f(x) = \frac{g(x)}{h(x)}$, find $f'(x)$.

   Solution: $f'(x) = \frac{[x^2 \cdot 1] - [(x+1) \cdot 2x]}{(x^2)^2} = \frac{-x^2 - 2x}{x^4} = \frac{-x - 2}{x^3}$.

2. If $g(x) = 3x$, $h(x) = 1 - x$, and $f(x) = \frac{g(x)}{h(x)}$, find $f'(x)$.

   Solution: $f'(x) = \frac{[(1-x) \cdot 3] - [3x \cdot (-1)]}{(1-x)^2} = \frac{3}{(1-x)^2}$.

3. If $g(x) = x^3 + 5$, $h(x) = x^3$, and $f(x) = \frac{g(x)}{h(x)}$, find $f'(x)$.

Solution: $f'(x) = \frac{[x^3 \cdot 3x^2] - [(x^3+5) \cdot 3x^2]}{(x^3)^2} = \frac{-15x^2}{x^6} = -\frac{15}{x^4}$.

POWER OF A FUNCTION (CHAIN RULE). If $f(x) = [g(x)]^n$, then $f'(x) = n[g(x)]^{n-1} g'(x)$.

The derivative of a function raised to a power is equal to the exponent times the function raised to the exponent minus 1 and all of that is multiplied by the derivative of the function.[2]

Examples:

1. If $f(x) = (25 - x)^{1/2}$, find $f'(x)$

   Solution: $f'(x) = \frac{1}{2}(25 - x)^{-1/2}(-1) = -\frac{1}{2}(25 - x)^{-1/2}$.

2. If $f(x) = (2x^2 - 3)^{3/2}$, find $f'(x)$

   Solution: $f'(x) = \frac{3}{2}(2x^2 - 3)^{1/2}(4x) = 6x(2x^2 - 3)^{1/2}$.

3. If $f(x) = (x^3 - 8x)^2$, find $f'(x)$

   Solution: $f'(x) = 2(x^3 - 8x)(3x^2 - 8)$.

2.5 SECOND DERIVATIVES*

The **second derivative** of a function is the derivative of the derivative of a function. If $y = f(x)$, the second derivative of $f(x)$ with respect to x is written as $f''(x)$ or d^2y/dx^2, and the same rules of differentiation apply.

Examples:

1. If $f(x) = 4x^2$, find $f''(x)$.

   Solution:
   Since $f'(x) = 4(2x^1) = 8x$, we have that $f''(x) = 8(1x^0) = 8$.

2. If $f(x) = x^{\frac{1}{2}}$, find $f''(x)$.

   Solution:
   Since $f'(x) = \frac{1}{2}x^{-\frac{1}{2}}$, we have that $f''(x) = -\frac{1}{4}x^{-\frac{3}{2}}$.

3. If $f(x) = x^3 + 200$, find $f''(x)$.

   Solution:
   Since $f'(x) = 3x^2$, we have that $f''(x) = 3(2x^1) = 6x$.

The second derivative, $f''(x)$, gives us the rate at which the *slope* of f is changing. Consequently, the second derivative is related to the *curvature* of the function. A function with a negative second derivative is *concave*. Figure 2.6 depicts such function. A concave function is "curved down," which can be seen by the fact that the slope of the function *decreases* as x increases (i.e., the tangent lines get flatter as x increases).

A function with a positive second derivative is *convex*. Since the function is "curved up," its slope *increases* as x increases (i.e., the tangent lines get steeper as x increases). Figure 2.7 depicts a convex function. A function with a second derivative equal to zero describes a *straight line*. Its slope *does not change* as x increases.

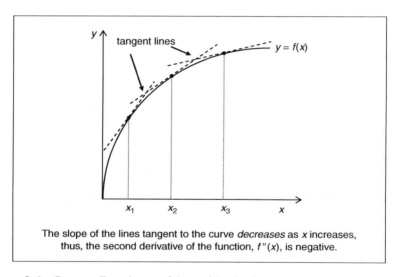

The slope of the lines tangent to the curve *decreases* as x increases, thus, the second derivative of the function, $f''(x)$, is negative.

Figure 2.6   Concave Functions and Second Derivatives

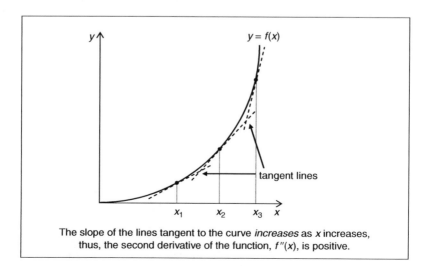

The slope of the lines tangent to the curve *increases* as x increases, thus, the second derivative of the function, $f''(x)$, is positive.

Figure 2.7   Convex Functions and Second Derivatives

Progress Exercises

1. Show (using derivatives) whether $f(x) = 3x^2 + 100$ is a concave or a convex function.

   Solution:

   It is a convex function since its second derivative is positive: $f'(x) = 6x$ and $f''(x) = 6 > 0$.

2. Show (using derivatives) whether $f(x) = 3\sqrt{x} + 2$ is a concave or a convex function.

   Solution:

   It is a concave function since its second derivative is negative: $f'(x) = \frac{3}{2}x^{-\frac{1}{2}}$ and $f''(x) = -\frac{3}{4}x^{-\frac{3}{2}} = -\frac{3}{4} \cdot \frac{1}{\sqrt{x^3}} = -\frac{3}{4} \cdot \frac{1}{x\sqrt{x}} < 0$.

3. Show (using derivatives) whether $f(x) = 3x - 1$ is a concave or a convex function.

   Solution:

   This is neither a concave nor a convex function. It is a straight line. Its second derivative is zero since its slope never changes: $f'(x) = 3$ and $f''(x) = 0$.

Application 2.3   Diminishing Marginal Utility

Consider a simple scenario in which a consumer, Joe, purchases only one good, pizzas. Let $U(x)$ denote the level of satisfaction or utility that he derives from purchasing x number of pizzas. Suppose, in particular, that Joe's utility function from consuming x pizzas is given by:

$$U(x) = \sqrt{x}. \qquad (2.2)$$

Panel A in figure 2.8 depicts this utility function.

   The *marginal utility*, MU, measures the additional satisfaction obtained from consuming one additional pizza. Mathematically, it is given by the derivative of the utility function,

$$MU = U'(x).$$

   Joe's utility increases with every additional pizza he consumes. For example, when he consumes 4 pizzas, he gets a utility of $U(4) = \sqrt{4} = 2$ (point *m*) and when he consumes 9, he gets a utility of $U(9) = \sqrt{9} = 3$ (point *n*). Since Joe's utility increases as his level of consumption rises, his marginal utility, MU, is positive ($U'(x) > 0$). We verify this by taking the derivative of equation (2.2):

$$MU = U'(x) = \frac{1}{2} \cdot \frac{1}{\sqrt{x}} > 0.$$

Graphically, the marginal utility at a particular point is the slope of a line tangent to the utility function at that point.

However, the more pizza Joe consumes, the less *additional* satisfaction that he gets from *additional* consumption ($U''(x) < 0$). This trend illustrates the principle of *diminishing marginal utility*. For example, when Joe consumes 4 pizzas, his marginal utility is $U'(4) = 0.25$ (slope at point *m*) and when he consumes 9, his marginal utility is $U'(9) = 0.17$ (slope at point *n*). Panel B of figure 2.8 depicts the marginal utility curve for this example.

Diminishing marginal utility implies that the more pizzas Joe has already consumed, the less additional satisfaction he will receive from an additional pizza. To verify this property, we can take the second derivative of equation

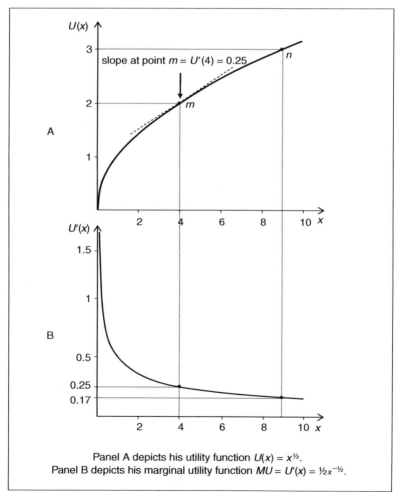

Panel A depicts his utility function $U(x) = x^{1/2}$.
Panel B depicts his marginal utility function $MU = U'(x) = \frac{1}{2}x^{-1/2}$.

Figure 2.8 Joe's Utility and Marginal Utility

(2.2) and find that this is indeed negative:

$$U''(x) = -\frac{1}{4} \cdot \frac{1}{\sqrt{x^3}} = -\frac{1}{4} \cdot \frac{1}{x\sqrt{x}} < 0.$$

2.6 PARTIAL DERIVATIVES*

Suppose that y is a function that depends on two variables, x and z, so that $y = f(x, z)$. The **partial derivative** tells us how the function changes as we change one variable alone, holding all other variables constant. Since $f(x, z)$ has two variables, it will have two partial derivatives: a partial derivative with respect to x and a partial derivative with respect to z. The partial derivative with respect to x is the derivative of the function with respect to x, *holding z fixed*. Similarly, the partial derivative with respect to z holds x fixed.

Partial derivatives follow the same rules as ordinary derivatives, and all the variables other than the one being differentiated with respect to are treated as *constants*. The notation, however, is slightly different. We can no longer use $f'(x, z)$ because it would not be clear with respect to which variable we are differentiating. Instead, we can use a subscript to make this distinction. Hence, $f_x(x, z)$ represents the partial derivative with respect to x, and $f_z(x, z)$ represents the partial derivative with respect to z.

An alternative notation for partial derivatives involves the use of the symbol ∂. In this case, we use $\frac{\partial f(x, z)}{\partial x}$ to indicate the partial derivative of f with respect to x and $\frac{\partial f(x, z)}{\partial z}$ to indicate the partial derivate of f with respect to z. Note that $\frac{\partial f(x, z)}{\partial z}$ is not a fraction, it is a single symbol for partial derivative. This is the notation that we will be using for partial differentiation.

Examples:

1. If $f(x, z) = 4x^2 + 3zx$, find $\frac{\partial f(x, z)}{\partial x}$ and $\frac{\partial f(x, z)}{\partial z}$.

   Solution:

   $\frac{\partial f(x, z)}{\partial x} = 8x + 3z\left(1x^0\right) = 8x + 3z$ (treat the variable z as if it were a constant).

   $\frac{\partial f(x, z)}{\partial z} = 0 + 3x\left(1z^0\right) = 3x$ (treat the variable x as if it were a constant).

2. If $f(x, w, z) = 5x + xz^3 - 8zw^2$, find $\frac{\partial f(x, w, z)}{\partial x}$, $\frac{\partial f(x, w, z)}{\partial w}$, and $\frac{\partial f(x, w, z)}{\partial z}$.

   Solution:

   $\frac{\partial f(x, w, z)}{\partial x} = 5\left(1x^0\right) + z^3\left(1x^0\right) - 0 = 5 + z^3$ (treat z and w as if they were constants).

   $\frac{\partial f(x, w, z)}{\partial w} = 0 + 0 - 8z\left(2w^1\right) = -16zw$ (treat x and z as if they were constants).

$\frac{\partial f(x,w,z)}{\partial z} = 0 + x\left(3z^2\right) - 8w^2\left(1z^0\right) = 3xz^2 - 8w^2$ (treat x and w as if they were constants).

3. If $q(K, L) = 4K^{0.5}L^{0.5}$, find $\frac{\partial q(K,L)}{\partial K}$ and $\frac{\partial q(K,L)}{\partial L}$.

Solution:

$\frac{\partial q(K,L)}{\partial K} = 4L^{0.5}\left(0.5K^{-0.5}\right) = 2\frac{L^{0.5}}{K^{0.5}} = 2\left(\frac{L}{K}\right)^{0.5}$.

$\frac{\partial q(K,L)}{\partial L} = 4K^{0.5}\left(0.5L^{-0.5}\right)2\frac{K^{0.5}}{L^{0.5}} = 2\left(\frac{K}{L}\right)^{0.5}$.

Application 2.4   Partial Derivatives and the Ceteris Paribus Assumption
The *ceteris paribus* assumption, which means "all other things equal," is frequently used in economics. The ceteris paribus assumption is represented in mathematical terms by the use of partial differentiation. For example, the demand curve shows the relationship between price p and quantity demanded Q^d assuming that all other variables that influence demand (price of alternative goods p_a and income I) are being held constant. The mathematical statement "$\partial Q^d/\partial p < 0$" reflects the *law of demand*; it indicates that price and quantity demanded move in opposite directions when other factors that influence demand do not change.

Application 2.5   Income Elasticity of Demand
The *income elasticity of demand*, denoted by ε^I, describes how the quantity demanded responds to changes in income. In general, for a demand function $Q^d = D(p, p_a, I)$, the income elasticity formula is given by:

$$\varepsilon^I = \frac{\partial Q^d}{\partial I} \times \frac{I}{Q}.$$

The first part of this formula, $\partial Q^d/\partial I$, is the partial derivative of the demand function with respect to income. It tells us how quantity demanded changes when income changes assuming all other variables (i.e., p and p_a) are held constant. When we multiply this partial derivative by the ratio of income over quantity, I/Q, we obtain a unit-free measure.

The sign of this elasticity depends on the effect that income has on the demand of the good under analysis. If an increase in income leads to an increase in consumption, then $\partial Q^d/\partial I > 0$ and the income elasticity is positive, that is, $\varepsilon^I > 0$. Goods that have a positive income elasticity are called *normal goods* (food is typically a normal good).

If an increase in income leads to a reduction in demand, then $\partial Q^d/\partial I < 0$. Consequently, the income elasticity is also negative. Goods that have a negative income elasticity are called *inferior goods* (low quality goods are typically inferior goods).

Example 2.1: Calculating the income elasticity of demand
Suppose that demand for newspapers is given by

$$Q_n^d = 70 - 4p_n + 4p_m + 2I$$

and supply is given by

$$Q_n^s = 100 + 6p_n,$$

where the subscript n stands for newspapers, the subscript m stands for magazines, and I stands for income.

a) Suppose that $p_m = 5$ and $I = 25$. What is the equilibrium price and quantity of newspapers?
b) Calculate the income elasticity of newspapers at this equilibrium. Are newspapers a normal or inferior good?

Solution:

a) Substituting the information given, $p_m = 5$ and $I = 25$, into the demand we get

$$Q_n^d = 140 - 4p_n.$$

Then, we set demand equal to supply to get the equilibrium price,

$$140 - 4p_n = 100 + 6p_n.$$

Solving for price we get $p_n^* = 4$. Then, substitute into either the supply or demand to get the equilibrium quantity, $Q_n^* = 124$.
b) The income elasticity at this equilibrium is given by:

$$\varepsilon^I = \frac{\partial Q_n^d}{\partial I} \times \frac{I}{Q_n^*} = 2 \times \frac{25}{124} = 0.4.$$

This elasticity is positive, which means that demand for newspapers rises as consumer income goes up. This indicates that newspapers are a normal good.

2.7 OPTIMIZATION

The calculus approach to optimization problems uses the derivatives of a function to find where a function reaches a *maximum* or a *minimum*. By **optimization**, we mean finding the maximum or the minimum of a function called the *objective function*.

The optimization problem faced by the decision maker is an **unconstrained optimization** problem if there are no limitations or restrictions on the possible choices. The optimization problem is a **constrained optimization** problem when there are imposed limits or restrictions on the possible choices.

2.7.1 Unconstrained Optimization

Consider the function $y = f(x)$, the function achieves a **maximum** at x^* if $f(x^*) \geq f(x)$ for all x. It can be shown that if $f(x)$ is a smooth function that achieves a maximum value at x^* then,

$$f'(x^*) = 0 \tag{2.3}$$
$$f''(x^*) < 0. \tag{2.4}$$

Expression (2.3) is called the **first-order** (necessary) **condition** (FOC) for a maximum. The FOC says that at the maximum, the derivative of the function must equal zero. Graphically, the FOC says that the function is flat at x^*. That is, as illustrated in figure 2.9, the slope of the function must be equal to zero at this point.

Expression (2.4) is called the **second-order** (sufficient) **condition** (SOC) for a maximum. The SOC is based on the second derivative of the function. If x^* is a maximum, the second derivative of the function evaluated at x^* must be negative. The SOC says that the function is concave near x^*. The SOC is sufficient in the sense that when combined with the FOC, the two jointly guarantee a maximum.

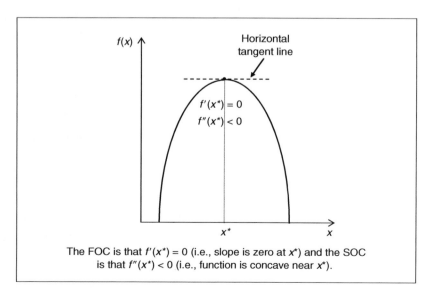

The FOC is that $f'(x^*) = 0$ (i.e., slope is zero at x^*) and the SOC is that $f''(x^*) < 0$ (i.e., function is concave near x^*).

Figure 2.9 First and Second Order Conditions for a Maximum

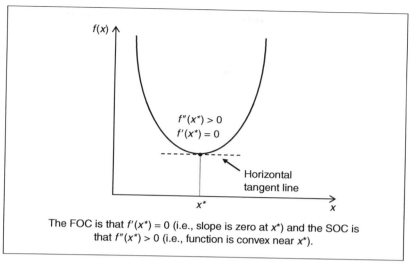

The FOC is that $f'(x^*) = 0$ (i.e., slope is zero at x^*) and the SOC is that $f''(x^*) > 0$ (i.e., function is convex near x^*).

Figure 2.10 First and Second Order Conditions for a Minimum

We say that the function $f(x)$ achieves its **minimum** value at x^* if $f(x^*) \leq f(x)$ for all x. If $f(x)$ is a smooth function that achieves a minimum value at x^*, then

$$f'(x^*) = 0 \qquad (2.5)$$
$$f''(x^*) > 0. \qquad (2.6)$$

Expression (2.5) is the FOC; it states that the function is flat at x^*. As illustrated in figure 2.10, the slope of the function must be equal to zero at this point.

Expression (2.6) is the SOC for a minimum; it states that if x^* is a minimum, the second derivative of the function evaluated at x^* must be positive. The SOC says that the function is convex near x^*.

Examples:

1. Find the value x^* that maximizes the function $f(x) = 50x - x^2$. Verify through the SOC that this value is indeed a maximum.

   Solution:

   To find the value x^* at which the function is maximized, we get the FOC by taking the derivative of the function and setting it equal to zero.

   $$\text{FOC: } f'(x^*) = 50 - 2x^* = 0.$$

   Solving for x^* gives us $x^* = 25$.

We now verify through the SOC that $x^* = 25$ is indeed a maximum.

$$\text{SOC: } f''(x^*) = -2 < 0.$$

The second derivative is smaller than zero. Since both the FOC and SOC hold, we can conclude that $x^* = 25$ is indeed a maximum.

2. Find the value x^* that minimizes the function $f(x) = \frac{2}{x} + 0.5x$. Verify through the SOC that this value is indeed a minimum.

Solution:

To find the value x^* at which the function is minimized, we get the FOC by taking the derivative of the function and setting it equal to zero.

$$\text{FOC: } f'(x^*) = -\frac{2}{x^{2*}} + 0.5 = 0.$$

Solving for x^* gives us $x^* = 2$.

We now verify, through the SOC, that $x^* = 2$ is indeed a minimum.

$$\text{SOC: } f''(2) = 4x^{-3} = \frac{4}{2^3} = \frac{1}{2} > 0.$$

The second derivative evaluated at $x^* = 2$ is larger than zero. Since both the FOC and SOC hold, we can be sure this is a minimum.

3. Find the value x^* that maximizes the function $f(x) = 16x - x^2$. Verify through the SOC that this value is indeed a maximum.

Solution:

To find the value x^* at which the function is maximized, we get the FOC by taking the derivative of the function and setting it equal to zero.

$$\text{FOC: } f'(x^*) = 16 - 2x^* = 0.$$

Solving for x^* gives us $x^* = 8$.

We now verify, through the SOC, that $x^* = 8$ is indeed a maximum.

$$\text{SOC: } f''(x^*) = -2 < 0.$$

The second derivative is smaller than zero. Since both the FOC and SOC hold, we can be sure this is a maximum.

Application 2.6   Profit Maximization

Consider a firm that sells output q. The firm's objective is to choose the level of output q^* that maximizes profits which we denote by Π (pi). More formally, the firm's problem is:

$$\max_{q} \Pi(q). \tag{2.7}$$

To find the value q^* at which the profit function is maximized, we need to get the FOC by taking the derivative of the function and setting it equal to zero.

$$\text{FOC: } \Pi'(q^*) = 0. \tag{2.8}$$

What follows is to verify through the SOC that q^* is a maximum. The SOC for problem (2.7) is

$$\text{SOC: } \Pi''(q^*) < 0, \tag{2.9}$$

where $\Pi''(q^*)$ is the second derivative of the profit function evaluated at q^*. With these general results in mind, let's now examine a specific numerical example.

Example 2.2: Profit maximization for a particular firm
Suppose that a firm's profit function is given by

$$\Pi(q) = 30q - q^2,$$

and that the objective of the firm is to find the value q^* that maximizes profits. This profit function is depicted in figure 2.11.

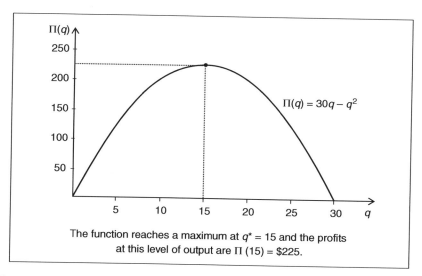

The function reaches a maximum at $q^* = 15$ and the profits at this level of output are $\Pi(15) = \$225$.

Figure 2.11   Example 2.2 Maximizing Profits

To find the value q^* at which the function is maximized, we need to get the FOC by taking the derivative of the function and setting it equal to zero.

$$\text{FOC: } \Pi'(q^*) = 30 - 2q^* = 0. \tag{2.10}$$

The solution to equation (2.10) is $q^* = 15$.

We now verify, through the SOC, that $q^* = 15$ is indeed a maximum. To get the SOC, we take the derivative of equation (2.10)

$$\text{SOC: } \Pi''(q^*) = -2 < 0.$$

The second derivative is smaller than zero.

Since both the FOC and SOC hold, we can conclude that the level of output that maximizes profits for this firm is $q^* = 15$. At this level of output, profits are equal to $\Pi(15) = (30 \times 15) - 15^2 = \$225$.

TEST YOUR UNDERSTANDING 3

Suppose that a firm's profit function is given by $\Pi(q) = 1,000q - 5q^2$. Find the value q^* that maximizes the firm's profits.

(*Solution are in Appendix B*)

2.7.2 *Constrained Optimization**

A constrained optimization problem finds the maximum or minimum of some function $f(x, z)$ over some restricted values of (x, z). In particular, the notation

$$\max_{x,z} f(x, z)$$

subject to $g(x, z) = 0$

means: find x^* and z^* such that $f(x^*, z^*) \geq f(x, z)$ for all values of x and z that satisfy the equation $g(x, z) = 0$.

The function $f(x, z)$ is called the **objective function**. The x and z are called **choice variables** and are usually written beneath the operator "max" to remind us that it is the values of x and z that we seek. If this were a minimization problem, the only difference is that we would have the operator "min" instead. The equation $g(x, z) = 0$ is called the **constraint**, and it jointly specifies those values of the choice variables that are considered *feasible* in solving the problem.

There are two ways to solve a constrained optimization problem:

METHOD 1. The first way is to solve the constraint for one of the choice variables in terms of the other and then substitute this into the objective function. The problem then turns into an unconstrained optimization problem in one variable.

METHOD 2. The second way to solve a constrained optimization problem is through the use of **Lagrange multipliers**.

The following application and a numerical example are used to illustrate both methods of solving constrained optimization problems.

Application 2.7   Consumer's Utility Maximization Problem

The consumer wants to choose the combination of good x and good z that maximize her utility function, $U(x, z)$. However, she has only certain income I to spend and faces the corresponding prices for the goods p_x and p_z. Thus, we can write the *consumer's utility maximization problem* as follows:

$$\max_{x,z} U(x, z)$$

subject to $p_x x + p_z z = I$.

This problem asks us to choose the values of x and z that, first, satisfy the consumer's budget constraint and, second, give us the larger value of $U(x, z)$ than any other values of x and z that satisfy the constraint.

METHOD 1. The first step is to solve the budget constraint for either one of the variables. If we choose to solve the constraint for z in terms of x, for example, we get:

$$z = \frac{I}{p_z} - \frac{p_x}{p_z} x. \tag{2.11}$$

Next, we substitute the right-hand side of equation (2.11) wherever z appears in the utility function to get the following unconstrained maximization problem:

$$\max_{x} U\left(x, \frac{I}{p_z} - \frac{p_x}{p_z} x\right). \tag{2.12}$$

The consumer's problem is now to maximize the utility function in (2.12) by the choice of x. Any value x^* that solves the problem must satisfy the FOC that we get by taking the derivative of the function and setting it equal to zero.

METHOD 2. The second technique to solve this constrained optimization problem is through the use of Lagrange multipliers. This method starts by defining an auxiliary function known as the *Lagrangian function*, denoted by $L(\cdot)$. The Lagrangian function has three variables x, z, and λ:

$$L(x, z, \lambda) = U(x, z) + \lambda\left(I - p_x x - p_z z\right).$$

The new variable λ (lamda) is called a Lagrange multiplier. Lagrange's theorem says that an optimal choice, (x^*, z^*), must satisfy the following three first-order conditions:

$$\text{FOC:} \quad \frac{\partial L}{\partial x} = \frac{\partial U(x^*, z^*)}{\partial x} - \lambda p_x = 0, \tag{2.13}$$

$$\frac{\partial L}{\partial z} = \frac{\partial U(x^*, z^*)}{\partial z} - \lambda p_z = 0, \tag{2.14}$$

$$\frac{\partial L}{\partial \lambda} = I - p_x x^* - p_z z^* = 0. \tag{2.15}$$

Next, we can solve equations (2.13) and (2.14) for λ to get

$$\lambda = \frac{\partial U(x^*, z^*)/\partial x}{p_x} = \frac{\partial U(x^*, z^*)/\partial z}{p_z},$$

which after some simple algebraic manipulation gives us:

$$\frac{\partial U(x^*, z^*)/\partial x}{\partial U(x^*, z^*)/\partial z} = \frac{p_x}{p_z}. \tag{2.16}$$

Equations (2.15) and (2.16) give us a system of two equations and two unknowns that we can then solve to get the values of x^* and z^*. Let's consider an example to see how both techniques work.

Example 2.3: Jane's utility maximization problem
Consider a consumer, Jane, who purchases only two goods: good x and good z. She has an income of \$12 and the prices of the goods are $p_x = \$2$ and $p_z = \$1$ per unit. Suppose that Jane's utility function is given by $U(x, z) = xz$. In this case, her utility maximization problem is given by:

$$\max_{x, z} U(x, z) = xz$$

subject to $2x + z = 12$

METHOD 1. Solving the constraint for z in terms of x, we get:

$$z = 12 - 2x. \tag{2.17}$$

Next, we substitute equation (2.17) wherever z appears in the utility function, and we get the following unconstrained maximization problem:

$$\max_{x} x(12 - 2x). \qquad (2.18)$$

We can then solve problem (2.18) by taking the derivative and setting the result equal to zero. This procedure will give us a FOC of the form:

$$12 - 4x^* = 0. \qquad (2.19)$$

Solving equation (2.19) gives us $x^* = 3$. To find the optimal quantity of good z, we simply substitute back into (2.17). This gives us that $z^* = 6$. So, the consumer's optimal basket is $(x^*, z^*) = (3, 6)$.

METHOD 2. Let's define the Lagrangian for this problem as:

$$L(x, z, \lambda) = xz + \lambda (12 - 2x - z).$$

Next, we get the three first-order conditions:

$$\text{FOC:} \quad \frac{\partial L}{\partial x} = z^* - 2\lambda = 0, \qquad (2.20)$$

$$\frac{\partial L}{\partial z} = x^* - \lambda = 0, \qquad (2.21)$$

$$\frac{\partial L}{\partial \lambda} = 12 - 2x^* - z^* = 0. \qquad (2.22)$$

Upon eliminating λ from equations (2.20) and (2.21), we find that

$$x^* = \frac{z^*}{2}. \qquad (2.23)$$

Then, we substitute (2.23) into (2.22) and find

$$12 - 2\frac{z^*}{2} - z^* = 0. \qquad (2.24)$$

Solving (2.24), we find that $z^* = 6$. Finally, we plug this value back into (2.23) to get $x^* = 3$.

2.8   EXPONENTIAL AND LOGARITHMIC FUNCTIONS

An **exponential function** is a function of the form

$$f(x) = b^x,$$

where b is a constant and $b > 0$, $b \neq 1$.[3] Note that in an exponential function, the variable x appears as the exponent (e.g., $f(x) = 2^x$), as opposed to a power function where x appears as the base (e.g., $f(x) = x^2$).

Although any number may be used as the base in an exponential function, one of the most common bases is the number e. The number e is an irrational number and is approximately equal to 2.718. Consider the exponential function given by $f(x) = e^x$, the following rules apply (e is for number e):

RULE 1e. e^x is always positive.

RULE 2e. e raised to any power can never equal zero, therefore, $e^x = 0$ has no solution.

RULE 3e. $e^0 = 1$.

As x gets smaller, the value of e^x approaches, but never reaches zero (mathematically, this is stated as "e^x is *asymptotic* to the x-axis on the left"). Figure 2.12 depicts the graph of $f(x) = e^x$. As you can see from the graph, as x gets large, e^x gets very large.

Application 2.8   Continuously Compounded Interest Rate

If money is invested at *simple interest*, the interest is paid only on the invested amount (i.e., principal). On the other hand, if money is invested at *compound interest*, at the end of the payment period, the interest due is reinvested at the same rate, so that the interest earned as well as the principal will earn interest during the next payment period.[4] In general, the value of a principal P, invested at an annual rate of r compounded m times a year at the end of

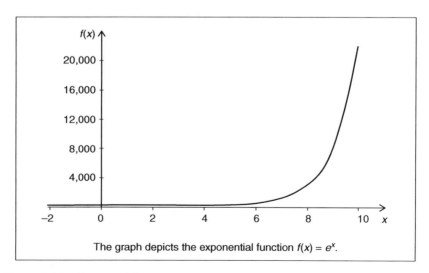

The graph depicts the exponential function $f(x) = e^x$.

Figure 2.12 Exponential Functions

t years, is:

$$P \times \left(1 + \frac{r}{m}\right)^{m \times t}.$$

Now, we say that the interest rate is *continuously compounded* when m, the number of times that the interest is compounded per year, is infinite. The value of a principal P, invested at a continuously compounded rate of r at the end of t years is:

$$P \times e^{rt}.$$

2.8.1 Logarithmic Functions

The inverse of an exponential function is called a **logarithmic function**. The expression $\log_b(x) = y$ is read "the logarithm of x to the base b is y." For a constant b where $b > 0$, $b \neq 1$, the logarithmic function is defined for $x > 0$ as:

$\log_b(x) = y$ if and only if $b^y = x$.

So, $\log_b(x)$ asks the question "to what power must you raise b to get x?" This means that the logarithm of a number is an exponent. For example:

$\log_2(8) = 3$ because $2^3 = 8$.

$\log_5(25) = 2$ because $5^2 = 25$.

$\log_3(9) = 2$ because $3^2 = 9$.

Any positive number can be used for the base b, but the two most frequently used bases are base 10 and base e. Logarithms to the base 10 are called **common logarithms**. With common logarithms, the 10 is omitted from the notation. In other words, if no base is written using logarithmic notation, like in $\log(x)$, the base is understood to be 10. The key labeled "log" (or "LOG") in your calculator represents a common (base 10) logarithm.

The following are some of the properties for common logarithms, for $x, z > 0$ (*log* is for common logarithm):

RULE 1log. $\log(1) = 0$

RULE 2log. $\log(10) = 1$.

RULE 3log. $\log(xz) = \log(x) + \log(z)$.

RULE 4log. $\log\left(\frac{x}{z}\right) = \log(x) - \log(z)$.

RULE 5log. $\log(x^z) = z\log(x)$.

2.8.2 The Natural Logarithm

When the number e is used as the base of a logarithm, we call it a **natural logarithm**. The expression $\ln(x)$ is read as "natural log of x." The natural

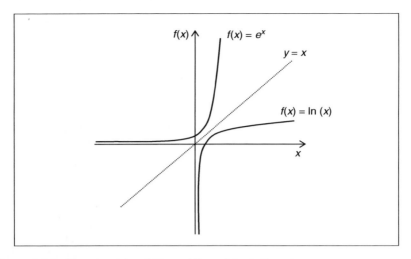

Figure 2.13 Exponential and Natural Logarithmic Functions

logarithm $\ln(x)$ is defined as follows:

$y = \ln(x)$ if and only if $e^y = x$.

The natural logarithmic function, $f(x) = \ln(x)$, has the following properties for $x, z > 0$ (*ln* is for natural logarithm):

RULE 1ln. $\ln(e) = 1$.
RULE 2ln. $\ln(e^x) = x$.
RULE 3ln. $\ln(1) = 0$.
RULE 4ln. $\ln(xz) = \ln(x) + \ln(z)$.
RULE 5ln. $\ln(x^z) = z\ln(x)$.

Figure 2.13 illustrates the relationship between the exponential function, $f(x) = e^x$, and the natural logarithmic function, $f(x) = \ln(x)$. The two functions are mirror images around the line $y = x$ (i.e., $45°$ line).

Application 2.9   Doubling Time for an Investment
A convenient way of comparing different investments is to use their *doubling times*, that is, the length of time that it takes for the value of an investment to double. Logarithms, as you will see in example 2.4, are very useful to simplify and solve doubling-time problems.

Example 2.4: Doubling time for an investment
Suppose that $500 is invested in a money market account that pays an annual interest rate of 5% compounded continuously. How long will it take for the money to double?

Solution:

We plug the information in the continuously compound interest formula discussed in Application 2.8:

$$500 \times e^{0.05t} = 1,000.$$

Our goal is to solve for t. First, simplify by dividing both sides by 500 and then apply natural logarithms to both sides to get:

$$\ln(e^{0.05t}) = \ln(2)$$
$$0.05t = \ln(2) \quad \text{(Apply Rule 2ln)}$$
$$t = \frac{\ln(2)}{0.05}$$
$$t = 13.9 \text{ years}.$$

So, we find that the doubling time of an investment of \$500 invested at 5% compounded continuously is approximately 14 years.[5]

2.8.3 *Differentiation of e and ln**

EXPONENTIAL RULE: The derivative of e raised to some exponent containing the independent variable equals the derivative of the exponent times the original function. In particular,

$$\text{if } f(x) = e^x, \quad \text{then } f'(x) = e^x.$$

Note that the exponent in this case is simply x and its derivative equals 1, so the derivative of the function is 1 times the original function.[6]

LOGARITHMIC RULE: The derivative of $\ln u(x)$ is the derivative of $u(x)$ divided by $u(x)$ itself. In particular,

$$\text{if } f(x) = \ln(x), \quad \text{then } f'(x) = \frac{1}{x}.$$

Note that in this case, $u(x) = x$, so $u'(x) = 1$.[7]

2.9 MEASURING AREAS UNDER LINEAR FUNCTIONS

Suppose that we wanted to calculate the area of the region bounded by the curve $y = f(x)$, the x-axis, and the lines $x = a$ and $x = b$ in figure 2.14. In this case, we would use a **definite integral** (provided f is continuous and $f(x) \geq 0$ on $[a, b]$).[8]

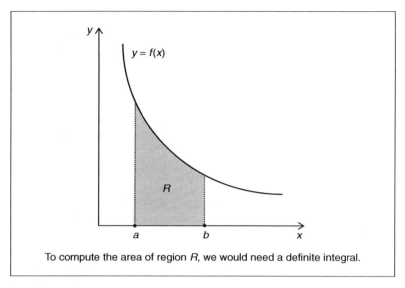

To compute the area of region R, we would need a definite integral.

Figure 2.14 Area under a Curve

When $y = f(x)$ is a linear function, however, this calculation typically reduces to computing **areas of triangles**. Let b denote the length of the base and h the length of the height; the formula for the area of the triangle is:

$$A = \frac{1}{2} b \times h.$$

Figure 2.15 illustrates this calculation graphically.

Application 2.10   Consumer Surplus

The **consumer surplus** tells us how much value a market creates for a consumer. It is the analogue of profit for the firm. One simple way to measure the consumer surplus from market purchases is by calculating the area under the demand curve and above the market price.[9]

The intuition behind this can be best understood by thinking of the market demand curve as being composed of many individual consumers' simple unit-demand curves. Each point on the curve represents a particular consumer's *reservation price,* which is the highest price that a given consumer will accept and still purchase the good. The fact that this reservation price is above the market price, p^*, implies that the consumer gets some surplus from the transaction. Adding up all of these rectangles, as illustrated in figure 2.16, gives us the area that represents the aggregate gains from trade.

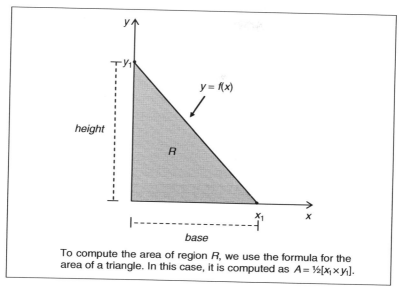

To compute the area of region R, we use the formula for the area of a triangle. In this case, it is computed as $A = \frac{1}{2}[x_1 \times y_1]$.

Figure 2.15 Area under a Linear Function

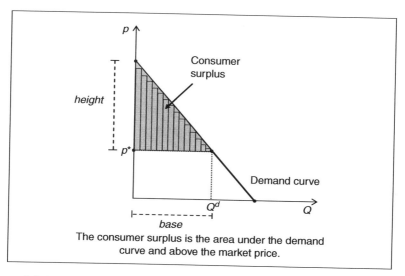

The consumer surplus is the area under the demand curve and above the market price.

Figure 2.16 Consumer Surplus

Example 2.5: Joe's consumer surplus

Joe needs to cross a bridge to go to work every day. The bridge charges a toll of \$2 per crossing. His weekly demand curve for bridge crossings is given by

$$p = 12 - 2q.$$

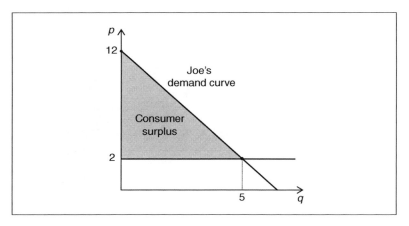

Figure 2.17 Example 2.5 Calculating Consumer Surplus

How much consumer surplus does Joe derive from crossing the bridge?

Solution:

If the price is $2, Joe crosses the bridge 5 times. So, we plug this information into the formula to get

$$CS = \frac{1}{2}[5 \times (12 - 2)] = \$25.$$

Figure 2.17 depicts the situation graphically to get a better understanding. Now, following the definition of consumer surplus—*area below demand curve and above price*—we can see that Joe's surplus is given by the area of a triangle with height of 10 and base of 5.

2.10   ECONOMIC MODELS

A **model** is a simplified representation of reality. Economic models illustrate, often in mathematical terms, relationships among variables.

There are two types of variables in a model: *endogenous* and *exogenous* variables. Variables are **endogenous** if their values are to be determined in the model and **exogenous** if their values are considered to be determined outside the model (i.e., they are taken as given).

Economists employ the notion of *equilibrium analysis*. Fundamentally, an **equilibrium** in a system is a state that will continue indefinitely, as long as every agent in the economy is doing the best they can and the exogenous variables remain unchanged.

2.10.1 Flow and Stock Variables

Economic variables that are measured per unit of time, such as per quarter or per year, are called **flow variables**. In contrast, economic variables that are defined at a point in time are called **stock variables**.

In many applications, a flow variable is the rate of change in a stock variable. A simple example that illustrates the relationship between a flow and a stock variable is a sink with water flowing from the faucet. The amount of water in the sink at any moment is a stock variable. Its units of measurement are, for example, gallons (without a time dimension). The rate at which the water enters the sink is the flow variable. Its time-dimensional units of measurement are, for example, gallons per minute.

Application 2.11   Balance Sheet and Income Statement
Understanding the distinction between stock and flow variables is particularly important when analyzing, interpreting, or preparing financial statements. A *balance sheet* reports the financial position of a firm at a particular point in time. That is, the balance sheet reports a firm's financial status as of certain date (e.g., at December 31, 2007). Hence, the items on the balance sheet—assets and liabilities—are stock variables.

In contrast, the *income statement* reports changes in the financial position of a firm over a period of time (e.g., for the year ended December 31, 2007). The items in the income statement—revenues and expenses—are flow variables.

2.10.2   Nominal and Real Economic Variables

Economic variables can be measured in *nominal* or *real* terms. Economic variables measured in terms of current market values are called **nominal variables.** Economic variables measured by prices of a base year are called **real variables**.

Application 2.12   Nominal and Real GDP
The broadest and most often used measure of aggregate economic activity is the *gross domestic product* or *GDP*. *Nominal GDP* is the sum of the quantities of final goods produced in an economy measured at their current market prices. Thus, nominal GDP changes over time for two reasons: because of changes in the quantities of the goods produced and because of changes in the prices of the goods.

If our intention is to measure production (quantities) and its change over time, we need to eliminate the effect of changing price levels. For this purpose, economists construct a measure of real GDP. *Real GDP* is the sum of the quantities of final goods produced in an economy measured using a constant set of prices (base-year prices).

Example 2.6: Nominal versus real GDP

Consider a simple economy that produces only two goods: computers and surfboards. Table 2.2 presents the data of this economy for two years.

We can calculate the nominal GDP of this simple economy in each year by adding the value of each good, that is,

$$GDP_1 = (100 \times \$200) + (2 \times \$1,000) = \$22,000$$
$$GDP_2 = (120 \times \$250) + (6 \times \$500) = \$33,000.$$

Note that the 50% increase in nominal GDP from year 1 to year 2 reflects changes in both quantities and prices.

To remove the effects of price changes, we measure the value of production using the prices from some *base year* (either year 1 or 2). Table 2.3 shows the data that we would need to calculate real output using year 1 as the base year.

In this case, real GPD in both years would be

$$GDP_1 = (100 \times \$200) + (2 \times \$1,000) = \$22,000$$
$$GDP_2 = (120 \times \$200) + (6 \times \$1,000) = \$30,000.$$

We are now able to calculate the increase in production (quantities) from year 1 to year 2. Because real GDP in year 2 is $30,000 and real GDP in year 1 is $22,000 (in the base year, nominal GDP = real GDP), output, as measured by real GDP, is 36.4% higher in year 2 than in year 1.

Table 2.2 Production and Price Data

	Year 1	Year 2
Quantity		
Surfboards	100	120
Computers	2	6
Price		
Surfboards	$200/board	$250/board
Computers	$1,000/computer	$500/computer

Table 2.3 Data for Calculation of Real Output with Base Year = Year 1

	Current Quantities	Base Year Prices
Year 1		
Surfboards	100	$200/board
Computers	2	$1,000/computer
Year 2		
Surfboards	120	$200/board
Computers	6	$1,000/computer

TEST YOUR UNDERSTANDING 4

Use the data of table 2.2 to calculate the growth in real GDP between the two years, but now, with the prices of year 2 as the base-year prices.

(*Solutions are in Appendix B*)

2.11   COMPARATIVE STATICS ANALYSIS

A **comparative statics** analysis involves comparing the equilibrium of a system before and after a change in an exogenous variable. We start with a system in equilibrium, then the system is perturbed by a change in an exogenous variable, and the system moves to a new equilibrium position. The results of our analysis are obtained by comparing the properties of the first equilibrium with the properties of the second equilibrium.

Application 2.13   Shifting the Demand and Supply Curves
Suppose that we have a market with a downward sloping demand curve and an upward sloping supply curve. Assume that such a market is initially in equilibrium, that is, demand and supply are equal. A comparative statics analysis involves looking at how the equilibrium price and the equilibrium quantity (endogenous variables) change as the demand or supply changes.

First, let's consider a change in demand. The demand curve shifts in or out if there is a change in the price of an alternative good (p_a) or a change in consumer income (I). These are the exogenous variables that affect demand (according to our discussion in application 1.2). Suppose that I increases, causing demand to increase.[10] In this case, as illustrated in figure 2.18 panel A, the demand curve shifts to the right (shifts out) while the supply is unchanged. The result of the demand increase is that both the equilibrium price and the equilibrium quantity rise.

Suppose instead that I falls, causing a reduction in demand. In this case, as illustrated in figure 2.18 panel B, the demand curve shifts to the left (shifts in) while the supply is unchanged. As a result of the demand reduction, both the equilibrium price and the equilibrium quantity fall.

Now, let's consider a change in supply. The supply curve shifts in or out if there is a change in the prices of the inputs (p_m) or a change in the price of technologically related goods (p_t). These are the exogenous variables that affect supply (according to our discussion in application 1.2). Suppose that p_m falls, causing supply to increase. In this case, as illustrated in figure 2.19 panel A, supply shifts to the right while demand is unchanged. The result of the supply increase is that the equilibrium quantity increases and the equilibrium price falls.

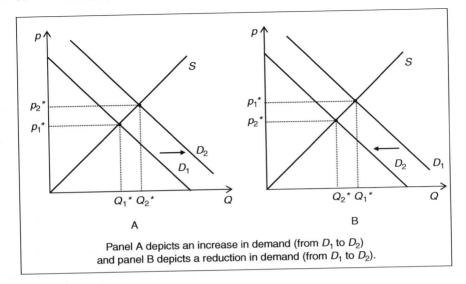

Panel A depicts an increase in demand (from D_1 to D_2)
and panel B depicts a reduction in demand (from D_1 to D_2).

Figure 2.18 Shifting the Demand Curve

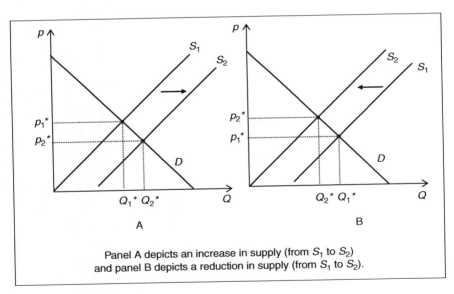

Panel A depicts an increase in supply (from S_1 to S_2)
and panel B depicts a reduction in supply (from S_1 to S_2).

Figure 2.19 Shifting the Supply Curve

Suppose instead that p_m rises, causing a reduction in supply. In this case, as illustrated in figure 2.19 panel B, supply shifts to the left while demand is unchanged. As a result of the supply reduction, the equilibrium quantity falls and the equilibrium price rises.

Practice Exercises

1. What is the derivative of the function $f(x) = 3 + 4x^2 - 5x$?
2. What is the derivative of the function $f(x) = 5x^2 - 4x^3 + x - 20$?
3. What is the derivative of the function $f(x) = 3 + \sqrt{x}$?
4. What is the derivative of the function $f(x) = 4x^2 - x^3 + 2x$?
5. What is the derivative of the function $f(x) = 125 - 33x + 0.5x^2$?
6. Consider the function $f(x) = x^2 - 2$. Find the slope of the line tangent to the function at the point where $x = 3$.
7. Consider the function $f(x) = 2\sqrt{x} + 55$. Find the slope of the line tangent to the function at the point where $x = 9$.
8. What is the second derivative of the function $f(x) = x^2 + 3x - 1$?
9. What is the second derivative of the function $f(x) = 4x^3 - 3x^2 + 17$?
10. Show (using derivatives) whether $f(x) = x^2 + 1$ is a concave or a convex function.
11. Show (using derivatives) whether $f(x) = \sqrt{x}$ is a concave or a convex function.
12. What is the partial derivative of the function $f(x, z) = 10 + 8x^2 - 5xz$ with respect to x and with respect to z?
13. What is the partial derivative of the function $Q(L, K) = L^{0.5}K^{0.5}$ with respect to L and with respect to K?
14. If $f(p, I, m) = 20 + 55m - p - 30I$, calculate the following partial derivatives: $\frac{\partial f}{\partial p}$, $\frac{\partial f}{\partial I}$, and $\frac{\partial f}{\partial m}$.
15. Find the value q^* that maximizes the function $\Pi(q) = 50q - q^2 - 15$ and verify (with the second order conditions) that this critical value is indeed a maximum.
16. Find the value q^* that minimizes the function $C(q) = 4q^2 - 16q + 20$ and verify (with the second order conditions) that this critical value is indeed a minimum.
17. Graph the equation $p = 10 - Q$ with the variable p on the vertical axis and calculate the area under the line. The variables Q and p can assume only nonnegative values.
18. Graph the equation $10Q = 20 - 5p$ with the variable p on the vertical axis and calculate the area under the line. The variables Q and p can assume only nonnegative values.
19. Graph the lines $p = Q$ and $p = 6$ with the variable p on the vertical axis and calculate the area between the two lines. The variables Q and p can assume only nonnegative values.
20. If the supply and demand functions in certain market are given by $Q^d = 30 - 2p$ and $Q^s = 4p$, find the consumer surplus (area below the *demand curve* and above the equilibrium price).

21. If the supply and demand functions in certain market are given by $Q^d = 21 - p$ and $Q^s = 2p$, find the consumer surplus (area below the *demand curve* and above the equilibrium price).

22. Suppose that a firm has a monthly cost of production given by

$$C(q) = 200 + 2q^2 - 36q.$$

Find the value q^* that minimizes the firm's cost and verify (with the second order conditions) that this critical value is indeed a minimum.

23. Suppose that a firm has a cost of production given by

$$C(q) = 3q^2 - 120q + 1,750$$

and that the firm's objective is to find the level of output q^* that minimizes costs. How much should the firm produce? What are the corresponding costs at this level of output?

24. Suppose that a firm's profit function is given by

$$\Pi(q) = 16q - 10 - q^2$$

and that the firm's objective is to find the level of output q^* that maximizes profits. How much should the firm produce? What are the corresponding profits at this level of output?

25. Suppose that a firm's profit function is given by

$$\Pi(q) = 8q - \frac{1}{2}q^2 - 2$$

and that the firm's objective is to find the level of output q^* that maximizes profits. How much should the firm produce? What are the corresponding profits at this level of output?

CHAPTER 3

Statistical Analysis Primer

The quantitative methods of statistical analysis allow us to transform raw data into useful information by developing numerical summaries, and revealing patterns, relationships, and trends, among others. Probability theory is the foundation on which statistics is built. It provides a means for modeling populations, experiments, and almost anything else that could be considered a random phenomenon. Through these models, one is able to draw inferences about populations, which are based on the examination of only a part of a whole.

3.1 ELEMENTS OF STATISTICS

A **population** includes all the objects of interest in a study. For example, all voters in a presidential election, all MBA applicants during a particular year, and all subscribers to a particular newspaper.

Suppose that we are interested in a particular attribute of the members of a population, such as, political preference, years of work experience, or salary. Obtaining the information for the entire population might be too costly and time consuming. Therefore, we often try to gain insight into the characteristics of a population by examining a *sample*.

A **sample** is a subset of the population. A good sample should be representative of its population of interest. This can be achieved if the sample is a *random sample*. A **random sample** is one where each unit in the population has the same chance of being included in the sample. After selecting a sample and collecting all the observations on the variable(s) of interest, the sample information is used to make **inferences** or predictions about the population.

We would typically want to summarize the information of our sample using **descriptive statistics**. The most commonly used descriptive statistics are

- Measures of central tendency (describe where the "center" of the data lies).
- Measures of variability (describe how spread out the data are).
- Measures of association (describe the linear relationship between two variables).

3.2 SIGMA NOTATION

Many of the formulas used in statistics (as well as in economics and finance) are expressed using *sigma notation*. So, before we start our discussion of descriptive statistics, let's review this notation.

The **sigma notation** (or **summation notation**) is typically used to express the sum of the n observations in a compact way. It is called sigma notation because the Greek letter Σ (sigma) is used as the summation sign. The lower limit of the sum is written underneath the summation sign and the upper limit of the sum is placed above it. For a sum from observation x_1 to observation x_n, the lower limit is $i = 1$ and the upper limit is n, and it is written

$$\sum_{i=1}^{n} x_i = x_1 + x_2 + x_3 + \cdots + x_n.$$

For example, suppose that we recorded the price of a certain stock (in dollars) for five days with these results:

Day	1	2	3	4	5
Price	10	13	15	8	9

Now, suppose that we are interested in calculating the average price of the stock during this five-day period. Let x_i denote the price of the stock on day i (e.g., if $i = 1$, we have x_1, which denotes the price of the stock in day 1, so, $x_1 = 10$). Using sigma notation, the average price is given by:

$$\frac{1}{5}\sum_{i=1}^{5} x_i = \frac{1}{5}(x_1 + x_2 + x_3 + x_4 + x_5) = \frac{1}{5}(10 + 13 + 15 + 8 + 9) = 11.$$

Now, for a constant c, we have the following rules for sums (s is for summation):

RULE 1s. $\sum_{i=1}^{n} cx_i = c\sum_{i=1}^{n} x_i$ (this means we can move the constant c out of the Σ sign).

RULE 2s. $\sum_{i=1}^{n} c = c\sum_{i=1}^{n} 1 = cn.$

Example 3.1: Sigma notation
Use the following table of values to evaluate each sum:

i	1	2	3	4	5
x_i	5	8	2	7	3

a) $\sum\limits_{i=1}^{5} \frac{1}{5}x_i$

b) $\sum\limits_{i=2}^{4} x_i^2$

c) $\sum\limits_{i=2}^{5} 2x_i$

d) $\sum\limits_{i=1}^{5} (x_i - 1)^2$

e) $\sum\limits_{i=1}^{5} 30$

Solution:

a) $\sum\limits_{i=1}^{5} \frac{1}{5}x_i = \frac{1}{5}\sum\limits_{i=1}^{5} x_i = \frac{1}{5}(x_1+x_2+x_3+x_4+x_5) = \frac{1}{5}(5+8+2+7+3) = 5$

b) $\sum\limits_{i=2}^{4} x_i^2 = x_2^2 + x_3^2 + x_4^2 = 8^2 + 2^2 + 7^2 = 117$

c) $\sum\limits_{i=2}^{5} 2x_i = 2\sum\limits_{i=2}^{5} x_i = 2(x_2 + x_3 + x_4 + x_5) = 2(8+2+7+3) = 40$

d) $\sum\limits_{i=1}^{5} (x_i - 1)^2 = (5-1)^2+(8-1)^2+(2-1)^2+(7-1)^2+(3-1)^2 = 106$

e) $\sum\limits_{i=1}^{5} 30 = 30\sum\limits_{i=1}^{5} 1 = 30 \times 5 = 150$

3.3 MEASURES OF CENTRAL TENDENCY

Measures of **central tendency**, as the name indicates, describe where the "center" of the data lies. Two of the most commonly used measures of central tendency for a quantitative data set are the *mean* and the *median*.

The **mean** is the average of the values of a variable. Suppose that we have a data set that consists of n observations, where x_i is the value of observation i. The **sample mean** is denoted by $\bar{x}$, which is read "x bar." The sample mean is calculated by first, adding all the observations, from the first observation, $i = 1$, to the last observation, $i = n$, and then dividing by n, that is,

$$\bar{x} = \frac{\sum\limits_{i=1}^{n} x_i}{n}.$$

The sample mean is typically used to estimate the **population mean,** denoted by the Greek letter μ (mu).

Now, suppose that we ordered all the observations in our data set from the smallest to the largest observation. The observation that is right in the middle of such list is called the **median**. If the data set has an odd number of

Table 3.1 Data Sets

Data Set 1	Data Set 2	Data Set 3
9	9	1
11	11	11
15	15	15
19	19	19
21	35	21
Mean = 15	Mean = 17.8	Mean = 13.4
Median = 15	Median = 15	Median = 15

measurements, the median is the middle number. If it has an even number of observations, the median is the average of the two middle observations.

To better understand the information provided by the mean and the median, let's compare the three simple data sets shown in table 3.1. The observations are ordered.

In data set 1, the observations are symmetric about the middle (one side approximately mirrors the other), so the mean and the median coincide. Data sets 2 and 3 contain one **outlier** observation, that is, a value that lies away from the rest of the data. In data set 2, there is an unusually large value (35) that pulls the mean up. Since this high observation does not affect the median (15 is still the middle value), the mean is above the median. Finally, in data set 3, the mean is below the median since the unusually small value (1) pulls the mean down without altering the median.

This example illustrates the merits of the two measures of centrality. The median is resistant to extreme observations. The reason is that those extreme values are not used in its computation. The mean, on the other hand, is sensitive to extreme observations. But, it does have the advantage of being based on information contained in *all* the observations of the data set.

Example 3.2: Measures of central tendency
Candy-Candy is a small candy shop located in downtown Chicago. Table 3.2 provides the daily sales information during three particular weeks.

Let's use the information in table 3.2 to calculate the mean and median of this data set. To calculate the mean, we simply need to divide the total weekly sales (sum of the daily sales) by seven (number of observations).

To calculate the median, the first step is to arrange the data from smallest to largest. In the table, the values are (conveniently) shown in such order and, since we have seven observations, the median is given by the fourth observation (i.e., Thursday's sales). Table 3.3 summarizes our results.

Note that for week 1, the mean and the median coincide since this data set is symmetric. In week 2, Monday's sales value is relatively low. This pulls the mean down and thus, the mean is below the median. Finally, in week 3, Sunday's relatively high value pulls the mean above the median.

Table 3.2 Candy-Candy Daily Sales
(Dollars, rounded to the nearest unit)

Day	Week 1	Week 2	Week 3
Monday	344	192	336
Tuesday	391	385	378
Wednesday	422	410	411
Thursday	450	452	455
Friday	491	481	470
Saturday	523	509	519
Sunday	529	546	707
Total weekly sales	3,150	2,975	3,276

Table 3.3 Candy-Candy Mean and
Median Daily Sales (Dollars, rounded
to the nearest unit)

	Week 1	Week 2	Week 3
Mean	450	425	468
Median	450	452	455

3.4 FREQUENCY TABLES AND HISTOGRAMS

Suppose that we have the following list with the ages of 30 students starting an MBA program.

28	24	28	24	35	29
21	31	22	27	30	29
31	32	30	34	32	27
33	34	22	26	25	29
26	28	25	23	27	28

To better understand this information, we can order the data and then graph it. To order the data, we use a *frequency table*. A **frequency table** lists the number of observations that fall into various specified equal-sized intervals, often called **categories**. A frequency table of the age data above could be, for example, as table 3.4.

The graphical representation of a frequency table is called a **histogram**. To construct a histogram, we draw a rectangle (bar) over each category. The height of the rectangle represents the frequency of observation for each category.

The value that occurs most frequently in the data set is called the **mode**. The mode can be determined by looking for the highest bar in the histogram.

Table 3.4 Frequency Table for Student Ages

Category	Frequency
21–23	4
24–26	6
27–29	10
30–32	6
33–35	4

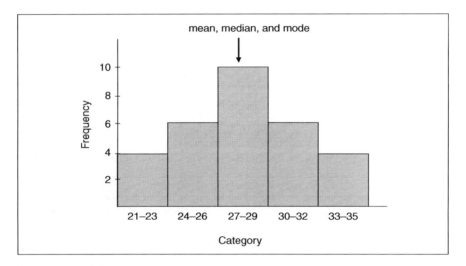

Figure 3.1 Symmetric Histogram

Let's look, for example, at figure 3.1, which depicts the histogram of table 3.4. We can see that the mode in this data set lies in the interval 27–29 years.

Histograms illustrate the nature of the distribution of a group of numbers. There are three general types of distributions: *symmetric*, *bimodal*, and *skewed*. The histogram depicted in figure 3.1 is **symmetric**, since it has a single peak and looks approximately the same to the left and to the right of the peak. Since the distribution is symmetric, the mean, median, and mode all coincide at the highest point, which is the middle of the distribution.

Let's verify the relationship between mean, median, and mode using the information in table 3.4. Suppose that we are only given the frequency table (and not the list itself). In this case, we typically assume that all ages in an interval are concentrated at the group's midpoint. Thus, the mode would be 28 years (midpoint of the interval 27–29).

To calculate the mean, let f_i be the frequency of x_i (i.e., the number of times age x_i occurs in the list), m be the number of age categories, and n be the total number of observations in the list. The formula for the mean is given by:

$$\bar{x} = \frac{\sum_{i=1}^{m} f_i x_i}{n}.$$

In our example, we have 5 age categories, so $m = 5$, and we have 30 observations, so $n = 30$. Thus, the expanded mean formula is

$$\bar{x} = \frac{\sum_{i=1}^{5} f_i x_i}{30} = \frac{(22 \times 4) + (25 \times 6) + (28 \times 10) + (31 \times 6) + (34 \times 4)}{30}$$
$$= \frac{840}{30} = 28.$$

Finally, the median is the average of the 15th and 16th observation. Since both these observations lie in the 27–29 interval, we know that the median is 28 years as well.

Now, consider a histogram like the one depicted in figure 3.2. This histogram has two peaks and its distribution is **bimodal**, that is, it has two modes. This is often an indication that the data come from two distinct populations. If the distribution is symmetrically bimodal, like in figure 3.2, then the mean and median coincide in the middle of the distribution. However, note that in this case, neither of them is a good indicator of a typical value.

A histogram is **skewed to the right** (or **positively** skewed) if it has a single peak and its longer tail is to the right of the peak. In this case, the mean will be larger than the median and the median will be larger than the mode. Figure 3.3 depicts an example of a positively skewed histogram.

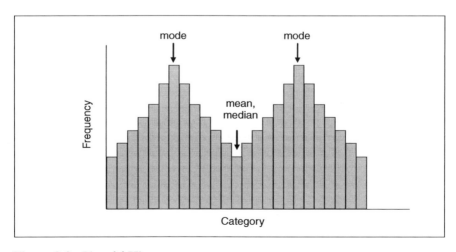

Figure 3.2 Bimodal Histogram

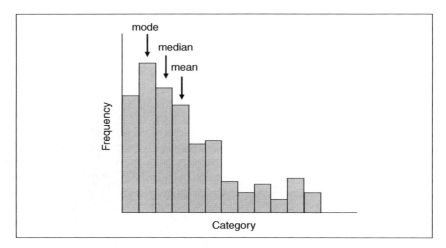

Figure 3.3 Positively Skewed Histogram (skewed to the right)

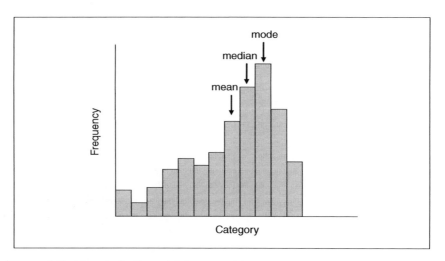

Figure 3.4 Negatively Skewed Histogram (skewed to the left)

A histogram is **skewed to the left** (or **negatively** skewed) if its longer tail is to the left of the peak. Figure 3.4 illustrates an example of such a histogram. In this case, the mode will be larger than the median and the median will be larger than the mean.

Example 3.3: Frequency tables and histograms

Table 3.5 is the frequency table of the GMAT scores of a sample of 80 MBA applicants to a certain business school.

Table 3.5 Frequency Table for Gmat Scores in Sample

Category	Frequency
550–600	10
601–650	12
651–700	15
701–750	19
751–800	24

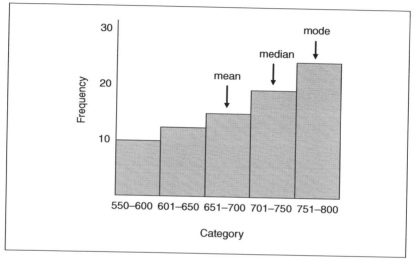

Figure 3.5   Example 3.3 Histogram for GMAT Scores

The histogram of this data is shown in figure 3.5. This histogram is skewed to the left or negatively skewed. We can see that the interval 751–800 has the highest bar in the histogram and thus, should contain the mode of the distribution. Assuming that all scores in an interval are concentrated at the group's midpoint, we can conclude that the mode is 775.5 points.

The median score is the average between the 40th and 41st scores. Both of these observations lie in the 701–750 interval, thus, the median is 725.5 points. Finally, using the formula for the mean, we have that

$$\bar{x} = \frac{\sum_{i=1}^{5} f_i x_i}{80} = \frac{\begin{matrix}(575 \times 10) + (625.5 \times 12) + (675.5 \times 15) \\ + (725.5 \times 19) + (775.5 \times 24)\end{matrix}}{80} = 697.3.$$

So, as expected, with a negatively skewed histogram, the mode (775.5) is larger than the median (725.5), and the median is larger than the mean (697.3).

3.5 MEASURES OF VARIABILITY

Measures of **variability** describe the spread of the data. The most common measures of variability are the *variance* and the *standard deviation*.

Suppose that we have a sample of size n and mean $\bar{x}$. We can compute the distance or **deviation** between every observation x_i and $\bar{x}$, that is,

$$x_1 - \bar{x}, \; x_2 - \bar{x}, \; x_3 - \bar{x}, \; \ldots, \; x_n - \bar{x}.$$

This set of distances contains important information. If the distances tend to be large, then the data are spread out, or highly variable. If the distances are mostly small, then the data exhibit low variability and are mainly clustered around $\bar{x}$.

Now, to condense the information on the distances from $\bar{x}$ into a single measure of variability, we cannot simply add these distances up and average them. If we did, the negative numbers and the positive numbers would cancel out, giving zero. So, what we do is we square these distances, making them all positive. The formula for the **sample variance**, s^2, is then given by

$$s^2 = \frac{\sum_{i=1}^{n} (x_i - \bar{x})^2}{n - 1}.$$

The sample variance is used to make inferences about the **population variance**, denoted by the symbol σ^2, which is read "sigma squared" (since σ is the lower case version of the Greek letter sigma).[1] Small variance means that the data are close to the mean, whereas large variance means large dispersion of the data.

A more intuitive measure of variability, however, is the **sample standard deviation**; denoted by *Stdev(x)* or s, and defined as the square root of the variance,

$$\text{Standard deviation} = \sqrt{\text{Variance}}.$$

The standard deviation is measured in the original units (as opposed to squared units) so, it is easier to interpret. The sample standard deviation is used to make inferences about the **population standard deviation**, denoted by σ. Just like with the variance, a small standard deviation means that the data are close to the mean and a large standard deviation indicates large data dispersion.

TEST YOUR UNDERSTANDING 1

(1) What is the smallest possible value of the variance?
(2) What are the units of the variance?

(*Solutions are in Appendix B*)

Table 3.6 Candy-Candy Daily Sales
(Dollars, rounded to the nearest unit)

Day	Week 1	Week 2
Monday	345	145
Tuesday	380	380
Wednesday	435	509
Thursday	510	702
Friday	440	522
Saturday	365	369
Sunday	325	173
Total weekly sales	2,800	2,800

Table 3.7 Measures of Variability of
Daily Sales

	Week 1	Week 2
Variance	4,200	39,314
Standard Deviation	$64.8	$198.3

Example 3.4: Measures of variability
Consider again the candy shop Candy-Candy. Table 3.6 provides the daily
sales information during two particular weeks.

As we can see from table 3.4, the average daily sales $(2,800/7)$ were the
same during both weeks, $400. However, the variability of the data is very
different. Using the formulas for sample variance and standard deviation, we
get the measures of dispersion presented in table 3.7.

What these results tell us is that, even though sales during both weeks were
centered at $400, the sales during week 2 were more spread out (lie farther
away from the mean) than those of week 1. In other words, there was more
variability in daily sales during week 2 than during week 1.

3.6 Measures of Association

Measures of association describe the linear relationship between two variables. The most common measures of association are the *covariance* and the
correlation.

To measure the association between two variables, x and y, these must be
paired variables, that is, we must have the same number of observations for
each of them. Typically, we would want to describe the behavior observed
between the variables in a graph called a *scatterplot*.

A **scatterplot** contains a point for each paired observation (x, y). Figure 3.6
illustrates an example of a scatterplot. This scatterplot, in particular, indicates
that there is a linear relationship between variables x and y. Furthermore, this

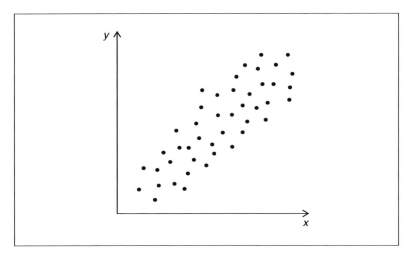

Figure 3.6 Scatterplot between Variables x and y

relationship seems fairly strong and positive. We will explore how to measure such relationship in more detail below.

Let x_i and y_i be the paired values for observation i, and let n be the number of observations. The **sample covariance** between x and y, denoted by $Cov(x, y)$, is given by

$$Cov(x, y) = \frac{\sum\limits_{i=1}^{n} (x_i - \bar{x})(y_i - \bar{y})}{n - 1}.$$

The covariance measures the direction of a *linear* relationship between x and y. It is an average of products of deviations from means. If x and y vary in the *same* direction—that is, when x is above (or below) its mean, y is also above (or below) its mean—the product of the deviations will be positive (since both deviations will be positive or both negative), so the covariance will be positive. If the opposite is true and x and y vary in *opposite* directions, the covariance is negative. The covariance, however, has the limitation of being affected by the units of measurement of the two variables.

The **sample correlation coefficient**, denoted by $Corr(x, y)$ or r_{xy}, measures the *strength* of the linear relationship between x and y. Unlike the covariance, the correlation coefficient is a unit-less quantity and its range of values is *always* between –1 and 1. It is calculated as follows:

$$Corr(x, y) = r_{xy} = \frac{Cov(x, y)}{Stdev(x) \times Stdev(y)}.$$

The sign of the correlation contains the same information as the sign of the covariance (in fact, they have the same sign since the standard deviations are always positive):

- *Positive sign* implies a *positive relationship*, *y* increases as *x* increases.
- *Negative sign* implies a *negative relationship*, *y* decreases as *x* increases.

Figure 3.7 depicts scatterplots of data sets where the variables display positive and negative correlations.

The correlation coefficient, however, is a better measure of the strength of the relationship:

- The closer r_{xy} is to 1, the stronger the linear relationship is with a positive slope.
- The closer r_{xy} is to –1, the stronger the linear relationship is with a negative slope.

Figure 3.8 panel A depicts a scatterplot where *x* and *y* are *perfectly correlated*, that is, $r_{xy} = 1$. Panel B of the same figure shows a scatterplot where *x* and *y* are *perfectly negatively correlated*, that is, $r_{xy} = -1$. The sample correlation coefficient, r_{xy}, is typically used to estimate the **population correlation coefficient**, denoted by the Greek letter ρ (rho). An important final remark regarding the correlation coefficient and the covariance is that both measure only the degree of association between the variables without telling us anything about causality.

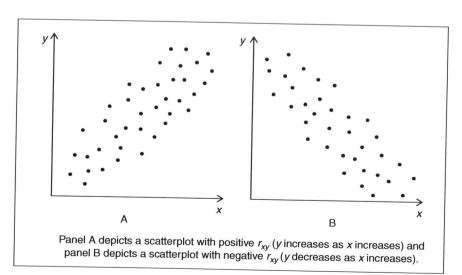

Panel A depicts a scatterplot with positive r_{xy} (*y* increases as *x* increases) and panel B depicts a scatterplot with negative r_{xy} (*y* decreases as *x* increases).

Figure 3.7 Correlation Coefficient

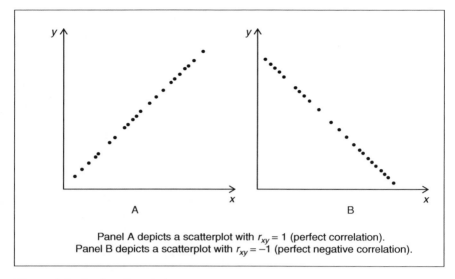

Panel A depicts a scatterplot with $r_{xy} = 1$ (perfect correlation).
Panel B depicts a scatterplot with $r_{xy} = -1$ (perfect negative correlation).

Figure 3.8 Perfect Correlation

TEST YOUR UNDERSTANDING 1

(1) If the sample correlation coefficient, r_{xy}, between x and y is equal to zero, does that mean x and y are unrelated?
(2) What is the covariance between a variable and itself (i.e., $Cov(x,x)$) equal to?

(*Solutions are in Appendix B*)

Example 3.5: Measures of association
Table 3.8 provides information on Candy-Candy's monthly sales and number of employees for a sample of nine months during particular year. We can use the information in table 3.8 to measure the relationship between the candy shop's sales force (variable x) and the monthly sales (variable y):

$$Cov(x,y) = \frac{\sum_{i=1}^{9} (x_i - 4.56)(y_i - 6,760)}{9 - 1} = \frac{23,056.12}{8} = 2,882.02$$

$$Corr(x,y) = r_{xy} = \frac{2,882.02}{1.67 \times 2,338} = 0.74.$$

What these results tell us is that Candy-Candy's sales force size (number of employees) and sales revenue are positively related. That is, when the number of employees goes up, sales revenue tends to go up as well. Furthermore, a correlation coefficient of 0.74 indicates that the positive relationship between

Table 3.8 Candy-Candy Monthly Sales and Employees

Month	Monthly Sales (Dollars, rounded to the nearest unit)	Number of Employees
1	3,569	3
2	3,003	2
3	7,166	5
4	5,847	4
5	7,998	6
6	6,994	7
7	7,091	3
8	8,963	5
9	10,207	6
Mean	**6,760**	**4.56**
St. Deviation	**2,338**	**1.67**

these two variables is strong (the maximum possible value for r_{xy} is 1). It is important to remember, however, that *correlation* does not imply *causality*. A change in sales revenues may be the result of many factors. We must be careful not to infer a causal relationship on the basis of high correlation. The only conclusion that we can make, based on the results of our sample data, is that a positive linear trend may exist between the number of employees and sales revenue.

3.7 PROBABILITY ESSENTIALS

Probability is a measure of the likelihood of some "event" (i.e., outcome) occurring. It is written either as a number between 0 and 1 or as a percentage. If the probability of an event is zero (or 0%), then it means the event will never occur, while an event with probability 1 (or 100%) will happen for sure.

To understand the basic intuitive idea behind the notion of probability, suppose there exists a finite set of possible outcomes (e.g., the total number of cards in a deck) and a certain subset of these outcomes has a particular property (e.g., being a spade). Then, the probability of this event, let's call it event A, is given by

$$Pr(A) = \frac{\text{outcomes with particular property}}{\text{total number of outcomes}}.$$

The expression "$Pr(A)$" is read "the probability of event A." For example, the probability of a spade being drawn from a deck of cards is $Pr(spade) = 13/52 = 1/4$.

We can also calculate the probability that event A will not happen as follows:

$$Pr(\text{not } A) = 1 - Pr(A).$$

For example, let's think of the probability of *not* drawing a spade. We know that either we draw a spade or not. Therefore, the probability of these two events must add up to 1. So, we have that $\Pr(not\ spade) = 1 - \Pr(spade) = 3/4$.

Examples:

1. What is the probability of drawing an ace from a deck of cards?

   Solution: $\Pr(ace) = \dfrac{4}{52} = \dfrac{1}{13}$.

2. If you toss a die, what is the probability that 5 is the number that appears on the die?

   Solution: $\Pr(5) = \dfrac{1}{6}$.

3. If you toss a die, what is the probability that 3 is not the number that appears on the die?

   Solution: $\Pr(not\ 3) = 1 - \Pr(3) = \dfrac{5}{6}$.

3.8 DISCRETE RANDOM VARIABLES

A **random variable** is an uncertain event. Random variables are defined in terms of outcomes and probabilities. Every outcome has an associated probability. There are two types of random variables, *discrete* and *continuous*.

Random variables are **discrete** if they can assume only finite, countable values. Examples of discrete random variables are: the *number* of customers waiting in a restaurant at a particular time, the *number* of patients seen by a doctor in a day, or the *number* of cars sold by a salesperson in a month.

Associated with each random variable is a **probability distribution** that lists all the possible values of the variable and the corresponding probabilities. These probabilities must be numbers between 0 and 1 and add up to 1.

We typically denote random variables with capital letters and use lowercase letters to denote the particular outcomes of the random variable. For example, the random variable X might be the number that appears if we toss a die, and $x = 3$ means that the number 3 appeared on the die. Table 3.9 shows the probability distribution of this random variable.

Table 3.9 Probability Distribution of X

x	$\Pr(X = x)$
1	1/6
2	1/6
3	1/6
4	1/6
5	1/6
6	1/6

Table 3.10 Cumulative
Distribution Function of X

x	$Pr(X \leq x)$
1	1/6
2	2/6 = 1/3
3	3/6 = 1/2
4	4/6 = 2/3
5	5/6
6	6/6 = 1

The first column of table 3.9 lists all the possible values that the variable X can have. The second column lists the probability of each event. Note that each probability is nonnegative (i.e., larger or equal to zero) and that the sum of the probabilities for all possible values equals 1.

Now, suppose that we are interested in the probability that the value of the random variable X is at most some value x. For example, if we let X be the number that appears on a die toss, we may want to find out the probability that the number showing on the die is smaller or equal to 4, that is, $Pr(X \leq 4)$.

The probability that the outcome of X is less than or equal to a given value is called the **cumulative probability** of X. We calculate the cumulative probability by adding up all the probabilities of the values of X that are less than or equal to x. In this example, the cumulative probability that X is less than or equal to 4 is:

$$Pr(X \leq 4) = Pr(X = 1) + Pr(X = 2) + Pr(X = 3)$$
$$+ Pr(X = 4) = 4/6 = 2/3.$$

Table 3.10 shows the **cumulative distribution function** or **cdf** for our example of rolling a die. Note that $Pr(X \leq 6) = 1$ because $Pr(X \leq 6)$ is the sum of the probabilities of all the values that are less than or equal to 6, and 6 is the largest value of this random variable.

Example 3.6: Discrete random variables
Suppose that an automobile dealership records the number of cars sold each day. Let X be the number of cars sold on a particular day. Table 3.11 shows the probability distribution of this discrete random variable.

a) Find the probability that the number of cars sold on a given day is between 2 and 4 (both inclusive).
b) Find the cumulative distribution function of the number of cars sold per day.

Table 3.11 Probability Distribution of X

x	$Pr(X = x)$
0	0.1
1	0.1
2	0.2
3	0.3
4	0.2
5	0.1

Table 3.12 Cumulative Distribution Function of X

x	$Pr(X \leq x)$
0	0.1
1	0.2
2	0.4
3	0.7
4	0.9
5	1.0

Solution:

a) $Pr(2 \leq X \leq 4) = Pr(X = 2) + Pr(X = 3) + Pr(X = 4) = 0.7$.
b) Table 3.12 shows the cdf for the number of cars sold daily.

3.8.1 Discrete Random Variables and Expected Value

Typically, we would want to summarize the information from a probability distribution with numerical measures like the *expected value* and the *variance*. Note, however, that these summary measures are based on probability distributions and not on observed data.

The **expected value** or the **mean** of X, denoted by $E(X)$ or by μ (mu), is the central tendency of the probability distribution. Intuitively, the expected value of a random variable tells you the average value of the variable if the "experiment" were repeated many times.

The expected value is calculated as a weighted sum of the possible values of X, using the probabilities as the weights. The formula for the expected value or mean of X is given by:

$$\mu = E(X) = \sum_{i=1}^{n} x_i \, Pr(x_i).$$

For example, let X be the number that appears if we toss a die. The expected value of this random variable is

$$E(X) = \sum_{i=1}^{6} x_i \Pr(x_i) = \left(1 \times \frac{1}{6}\right) + \left(2 \times \frac{1}{6}\right) + \left(3 \times \frac{1}{6}\right) + \left(4 \times \frac{1}{6}\right)$$
$$+ \left(5 \times \frac{1}{6}\right) + \left(6 \times \frac{1}{6}\right) = 3.5.$$

This number is the average value that we would have if we tossed the die (our experiment) many times.

3.8.2   Discrete Random Variables and Variance

To measure the variability in a distribution we calculate its variance and/or its standard deviation. The **variance** of X, denoted by $Var(X)$ or σ_x^2, is the weighted sum of the squared deviations of the possible values from the mean, using the probabilities as the weights. Deviations from the mean are squared to prevent positive deviations, weighted by their probabilities, from offsetting negative deviations.

The variance is given by the following formula:

$$\sigma_x^2 = Var(X) = \sum_{i=1}^{n} (x_i - E(X))^2 \Pr(x_i).$$

Since the formula for the variance uses squared deviations to make all the values positive, this alters the unit of measure to "square units." To transform the variance into the original units, we take the square root of the variance. This measure is the **standard deviation** of a random variable, denoted by σ_x, and calculated as,

$$\sigma_x = \sqrt{\sigma_x^2}.$$

Larger values of either the variance or the standard deviation indicate that the underlying random variable has a greater dispersion around its expected value.

Example 3.7: Probability, expected value, and variance
Suppose that an investor has a $100 worth of firm Green stock. Let X denote the investor's payoff. Assume that over the next year, this investment could be worth:

$$x_1 = \$75, \ x_2 = \$100, \ \text{or} \ x_3 = \$125.$$

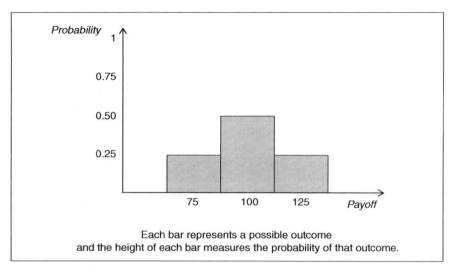

Each bar represents a possible outcome
and the height of each bar measures the probability of that outcome.

Figure 3.9   Probability Distribution of X

The x_i's represent the investor's payoff when event i occurs. Also, assume that the probabilities of each outcome are:

$$Pr(x_1) = \frac{1}{4}, \ Pr(x_2) = \frac{1}{2}, \ \text{and} \ Pr(x_3) = \frac{1}{4}.$$

Figure 3.9 illustrates the probability distribution of the discrete random variable X.

We can calculate the summary measures of X as follows:

$$E(X) = \frac{1}{4}(75) + \frac{1}{2}(100) + \frac{1}{4}(125) = \$100,$$

$$Var(X) = \frac{1}{4}(75 - 100)^2 + \frac{1}{2}(100 - 100)^2 + \frac{1}{4}(125 - 100)^2 = 312.50,$$

$$\sigma_x = \sqrt{312.50} = \$17.68.$$

Now, suppose that an alternative investment, firm Blue stock, becomes available. Let Y denote the investor's payoff. An investment of $100 worth of firm Blue stock over the next year could be worth:

$$y_1 = \$75, \ y_2 = \$100, \ \text{or} \ y_3 = \$125.$$

The y_i's represent the investor's payoff when event i occurs. The corresponding probabilities of each outcome are:

$$Pr(y_1) = \frac{1}{8}, \ Pr(y_2) = \frac{3}{4}, \ \text{and} \ Pr(y_3) = \frac{1}{8}.$$

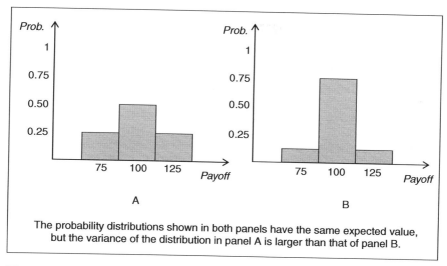

The probability distributions shown in both panels have the same expected value, but the variance of the distribution in panel A is larger than that of panel B.

Figure 3.10 Probability Distributions and Variance

How does the investment in firm Blue compare to the investment in firm Green?

To answer this, we need to calculate the summary measures of Y:

$$E(Y) = \frac{1}{8}(75) + \frac{3}{4}(100) + \frac{1}{8}(125) = \$100,$$

$$Var(Y) = \frac{1}{8}(75 - 100)^2 + \frac{3}{4}(100 - 100)^2 + \frac{1}{8}(125 - 100)^2 = 156.25,$$

$$\sigma_y = \sqrt{156.25} = \$12.5.$$

The expected value of the investment is the same for both firms (\$100). The investment in firm Blue, however, is less risky than that of firm Green since it has a smaller variance (or equivalently, a smaller standard deviation). Figure 3.10 compares the two probability distribution functions.

3.8.3   Decision Tree Basics

A **decision tree** is a diagram that describes the options and risks faced by a decision maker at each point in time. A decision tree, such as that illustrated in figure 3.11, has four basic elements:

- **Decision nodes**. A decision node, represented by a small bold square in the tree diagram, indicates a particular decision faced by the decision maker. Each branch from a decision node corresponds to a possible decision.

- **Chance nodes**. A chance node, represented by a small bold circle in the tree diagram, indicates an event faced by the decision maker; an event that has an uncertain outcome. Each branch from a chance node corresponds to a possible outcome.
- **Probabilities.** Each possible outcome has a corresponding probability. The sum of the probabilities of all the possible outcomes at a chance node must add up to 1.
- **Payoffs.** The end of each branch is located at the right end of the tree and has a payoff associated with it.

Example 3.8: Using a decision tree
The Chicago candy shop, Candy-Candy, is considering launching a new product line. The firm has two choices: a line of bonbons or a line of lollypops. Only one product can be launched. The project is risky, since the demand for each type of candy could turn out to be either high or low. Table 3.13 shows the firm's estimated payoffs for each potential product line.

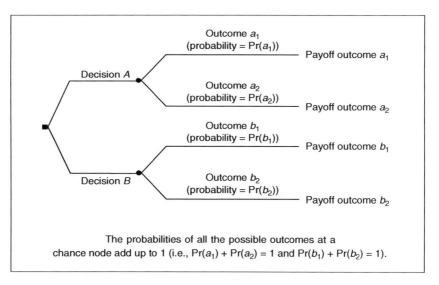

Figure 3.11 Decision Tree Diagram

Table 3.13 Candy-Candy Payoffs of New Product Line

Product	Outcome	Probability	Payoff (Dollars)
Bonbons	Demand is high	0.6	10,000
	Demand is low	0.4	−4,500
Lollypops	Demand is high	0.5	6,000
	Demand is low	0.5	3,000

Figure 3.12 illustrates the firm's decision tree.

The expected payoffs from launching each new product are:

$$E(\text{bonbons}) = (0.6 \times 10,000) + (0.4 \times -4,500) = \$4,200$$
$$E(\text{lollypops}) = (0.5 \times 6,000) + (0.5 \times 3,000) = \$4,500.$$

Figure 3.13 summarizes this information in a new (reduced) tree. The firm's manager can now easily identify that the optimal decision is to launch the lollypop line.

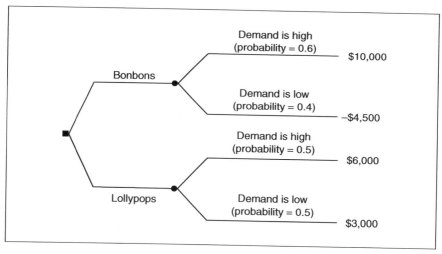

Figure 3.12   Example 3.8 Candy-Candy's Decision Tree Diagram

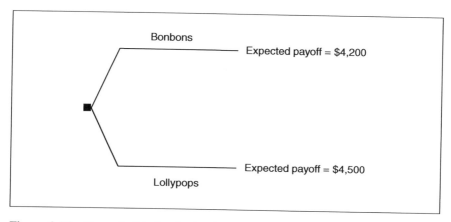

Figure 3.13   Example 3.8 Candy-Candy's (Reduced) Decision Tree Diagram

3.9 CONTINUOUS RANDOM VARIABLES

Random variables are **continuous** if they can assume any value within some interval. Examples of continuous random variables are: the *depth* to which a submarine can submerge, the *length of time* it takes to build a house, or the *weight* of a newborn baby.

Note that with a continuous random variable, we can no longer list all the possible values that the variable can take since there are infinitely many possibilities. Furthermore, since there is an infinite number of values, the probability that a continuous random variable X assumes a particular value x, for example, $\Pr(X = 3)$, becomes zero. So, our concern instead is the likelihood that X falls within an interval. For example, we would want to find $\Pr(X > 3)$ or $\Pr(X < 3)$.

We can geometrically represent the probabilities associated with a continuous random variable by means of the graph of a function $f(x)$. The function f is called the **probability density function** or **pdf** of X. To find probabilities from a density function we need to calculate specific areas under the curve, as illustrated in figure 3.14.

The area under the entire curve is 1, because the total probability of all possible values is always 1. Also, if X is a continuous random variable (CRV), we have the following results:

RESULT 1^{CRV}. $\Pr(X > a) = 1 - \Pr(X < a)$.
RESULT 2^{CRV}. $\Pr(a < X < b) = \Pr(X < b) - \Pr(X < a)$.
       Assuming that $a < b$ (as in figure 3.14).

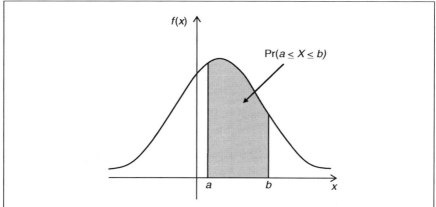

The area under the curve (and above the x-axis) and between the lines $x = a$ and $x = b$ represents the probability that X assumes a value between a and b.

Figure 3.14 Probability Density Function

RESULT 3^{CRV}. $\Pr(a < X < b) = \Pr(a < X \le b) = \Pr(a \le X < b) = \Pr(a \le X \le b)$.

The reason that we can be somewhat cavalier about the specification of the intervals is that, since X is a continuous random variable, $\Pr(X = x) = 0$.

We will expand on the methods to calculate probabilities of continuous random variables below.

3.9.1 The Normal Distribution

One of the most useful and frequently encountered continuous random variables has a **bell-shaped** probability distribution. The probability distribution of such a variable is called a **normal distribution** (or **Gaussian distribution**) and is shown in figure 3.15.

If X is a random variable that is normally distributed, has a mean of μ, and a variance of σ^2, we write it as $X \sim N(\mu, \sigma^2)$. The N stands for normal, and the symbol "$\sim$" is read as "is distributed as."

The normal distribution is perfectly symmetric about its mean, μ. This means that the area under the curve and to the right (or left) of μ is equal to $^1\!/_2$ (remember that the area under the entire curve is equal to 1).

The spread of the normal distribution is determined by the value of its variance, σ^2 (or equivalently, by its standard deviation, σ). Figure 3.16 illustrates how the value of σ affects the shape of the curve. A smaller variance/standard deviation (i.e., smaller σ) means that the probabilities are concentrated closer to the middle, which leads to a higher, narrower curve.

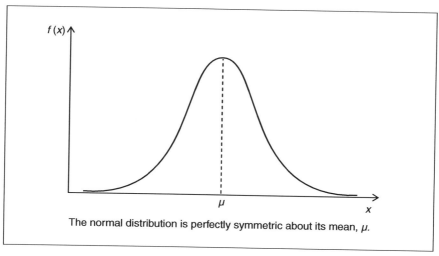

The normal distribution is perfectly symmetric about its mean, μ.

Figure 3.15 Normal Curve

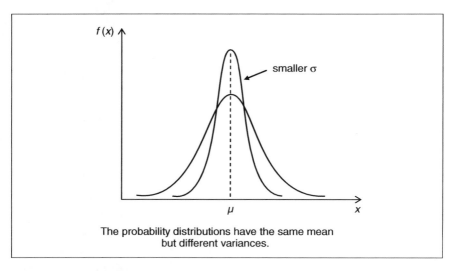

Figure 3.16 Mean and Variance

3.9.2 Standardizing: z-Values

The **standard normal variable** Z is a normally distributed random variable with mean of 0, and standard deviation of 1, that is, $Z \sim N(0, 1^2)$. If $X \sim N(\mu, \sigma^2)$, then the z-value corresponding to an x-value is:

$$z = \frac{x - \mu}{\sigma}. \tag{3.1}$$

This operation is called *standardizing*. The purpose of standardizing is to measure variables with different means and/or standard deviations on a single scale.

The z-value from operation (3.1) can be interpreted as the number of standard deviations that the value of x is to the right or left of the mean. If the z-value is positive, then the original x-value is to the right of the mean. If the z-value is negative, then the original x-value is to the left of the mean. For example, a z-value of 3 means that the original x-value is three standard deviations above the mean and a z-value of −2 means that the original x-value is two standard deviations below the mean.

3.9.3 Standard Normal Tables and z-Values

A common use for the z-values and the standard normal distribution is to calculate probabilities. Figure 3.17 depicts the standard normal curve. The entire area under the curve is 1, while the probability that a standard random variable lies within one standard deviation of the mean is approximately 68%, the probability that it lies within two standard deviations of the mean

STATISTICAL ANALYSIS PRIMER ✦ 109

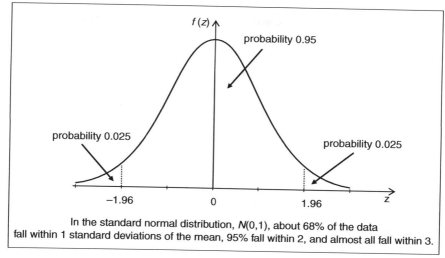

In the standard normal distribution, $N(0,1)$, about 68% of the data fall within 1 standard deviations of the mean, 95% fall within 2, and almost all fall within 3.

Figure 3.17 Standard Normal

is approximately 95%, and the probability that it lies within three standard deviations is approximately 99%.

We can obtain the values for the areas or probabilities of standard normal random variables from a variety of sources: tables, statistical software, calculators, among others. The traditional way of getting these probabilities is with the use of a table such as table 3.14. The body of this table contains probabilities. The left and top margins contain possible values of z.

Suppose, for example, that we want to calculate the probability that a standard normal random variable is less than 1.24, that is, $\Pr(Z < 1.24)$. We locate 1.2 along the left margin, and 0.04 (for the second decimal in 1.24) along the top margin, and then read into the table to find the probability of 0.8925. This means that the probability that the standard normal random variable is less than 1.24 is approximately 0.89. We can perform the same kind of calculations for any normal distribution by first standardizing.

Example 3.9: Normal distribution and z-values

1. Suppose that the variable X is normally distributed with mean of 150 and standard deviation of 25. Find the probability that X is less than 163.

   Solution:

   Applying the corresponding z-value, we have that

   $$\Pr(X < 163) = \Pr\left(Z < \frac{163 - 150}{25}\right) = \Pr(Z < 0.52).$$

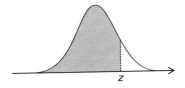

Table 3.14 Normal Probabilities

z	0.00	0.01	0.02	0.03	0.04	0.05	0.06	0.07	0.08	0.09
0.0	0.5000	0.5040	0.5080	0.5120	0.5160	0.5199	0.5239	0.5279	0.5319	0.5359
0.1	0.5398	0.5438	0.5478	0.5517	0.5557	0.5596	0.5636	0.5675	0.5714	0.5753
0.2	0.5793	0.5832	0.5871	0.5910	0.5948	0.5987	0.6026	0.6064	0.6103	0.6141
0.3	0.6179	0.6217	0.6255	0.6293	0.6331	0.6368	0.6406	0.6443	0.6480	0.6517
0.4	0.6554	0.6591	0.6628	0.6664	0.6700	0.6736	0.6772	0.6808	0.6844	0.6879
0.5	0.6915	0.6950	0.6985	0.7019	0.7054	0.7088	0.7123	0.7157	0.7190	0.7224
0.6	0.7257	0.7291	0.7324	0.7357	0.7389	0.7422	0.7454	0.7486	0.7517	0.7549
0.7	0.7580	0.7611	0.7642	0.7673	0.7704	0.7734	0.7764	0.7794	0.7823	0.7852
0.8	0.7881	0.7910	0.7939	0.7967	0.7995	0.8023	0.8051	0.8078	0.8106	0.8133
0.9	0.8159	0.8186	0.8212	0.8238	0.8264	0.8289	0.8315	0.8340	0.8365	0.8389
1.0	0.8413	0.8438	0.8461	0.8485	0.8508	0.8531	0.8554	0.8577	0.8599	0.8621
1.1	0.8643	0.8665	0.8686	0.8708	0.8729	0.8749	0.8770	0.8790	0.8810	0.8830
1.2	0.8849	0.8869	0.8888	0.8907	0.8925	0.8944	0.8962	0.8980	0.8997	0.9015
1.3	0.9032	0.9049	0.9066	0.9082	0.9099	0.9115	0.9131	0.9147	0.9162	0.9177
1.4	0.9192	0.9207	0.9222	0.9236	0.9251	0.9265	0.9279	0.9292	0.9306	0.9319
1.5	0.9332	0.9345	0.9357	0.9370	0.9382	0.9394	0.9406	0.9418	0.9429	0.9441
1.6	0.9452	0.9463	0.9474	0.9484	0.9495	0.9505	0.9515	0.9525	0.9535	0.9545
1.7	0.9554	0.9564	0.9573	0.9582	0.9591	0.9599	0.9608	0.9616	0.9625	0.9633
1.8	0.9641	0.9649	0.9656	0.9664	0.9671	0.9678	0.9686	0.9693	0.9699	0.9706
1.9	0.9713	0.9719	0.9726	0.9732	0.9738	0.9744	0.9750	0.9756	0.9761	0.9767
2.0	0.9772	0.9778	0.9783	0.9788	0.9793	0.9798	0.9803	0.9808	0.9812	0.9817
2.1	0.9821	0.9826	0.9830	0.9834	0.9838	0.9842	0.9846	0.9850	0.9854	0.9857
2.2	0.9861	0.9864	0.9868	0.9871	0.9875	0.9878	0.9881	0.9884	0.9887	0.9890
2.3	0.9893	0.9896	0.9898	0.9901	0.9904	0.9906	0.9909	0.9911	0.9913	0.9916
2.4	0.9918	0.9920	0.9922	0.9925	0.9927	0.9929	0.9931	0.9932	0.9934	0.9936
2.5	0.9938	0.9940	0.9941	0.9943	0.9945	0.9946	0.9948	0.9949	0.9951	0.9952
2.6	0.9953	0.9955	0.9956	0.9957	0.9959	0.9960	0.9961	0.9962	0.9963	0.9964
2.7	0.9965	0.9966	0.9967	0.9968	0.9969	0.9970	0.9971	0.9972	0.9973	0.9974
2.8	0.9974	0.9975	0.9976	0.9977	0.9977	0.9978	0.9979	0.9979	0.9980	0.9981
2.9	0.9981	0.9982	0.9982	0.9983	0.9984	0.9984	0.9985	0.9985	0.9986	0.9986
3.0	0.9987	0.9987	0.9987	0.9988	0.9988	0.9989	0.9989	0.9989	0.9990	0.9990
3.1	0.9990	0.9991	0.9991	0.9991	0.9992	0.9992	0.9992	0.9992	0.9993	0.9993
3.2	0.9993	0.9993	0.9994	0.9994	0.9994	0.9994	0.9994	0.9995	0.9995	0.9995
3.3	0.9995	0.9995	0.9995	0.9996	0.9996	0.9996	0.9996	0.9996	0.9996	0.9997
3.4	0.9997	0.9997	0.9997	0.9997	0.9997	0.9997	0.9997	0.9997	0.9997	0.9998
3.5	0.9998	0.9998	0.9998	0.9998	0.9998	0.9998	0.9998	0.9998	0.9998	0.9998

Then, we look up the value 0.52 in the table (0.5 row, 0.02 column) to find that the probability is $\Pr(Z < 0.52) = 0.6985$.

2. Suppose that the variable X is normally distributed with mean of 150 and standard deviation of 25. Find the probability that X is *more* than 172.

Solution:
Applying the corresponding z-value, we have that

$$\Pr(X > 172) = \Pr\left(Z > \frac{172 - 150}{25}\right) = \Pr(Z > 0.88).$$

Now, using RESULT 1^{CRV}, we have that

$$\Pr(Z > 0.88) = 1 - \Pr(Z < 0.88).$$

If we look up the value of 0.88 in the table (0.8 row, 0.08 column), we find that the probability Z is *less* than 0.88 is $\Pr(Z < 0.88) = 0.8106$. This means that the probability that Z is *more* than 0.88 is $\Pr(Z > 0.88) = 1 - 0.8106 = 0.1894$.

3. Suppose that the variable X is normally distributed with mean of 150 and standard deviation of 25. Find the probability that X is less than 97.
Solution:
Applying the corresponding z-value, we have that

$$\Pr(X < 97) = \Pr\left(Z < \frac{97 - 150}{25}\right) = \Pr(Z < -2.12).$$

By symmetry of the normal curve, the area to the left of -2.12 is exactly equal to the area to the right of 2.12, so we have that $\Pr(Z < -2.12) = \Pr(Z > 2.12) = 1 - 0.9830 = 0.017$.

4. Suppose that the variable X is normally distributed with mean of 150 and standard deviation of 25. Find the probability that X is *more* than 93 and *less* than 162.

Solution:
Applying the corresponding z-values, we have that

$$\Pr(93 < X < 162) = \Pr\left(\frac{93 - 150}{25} < Z < \frac{162 - 150}{25}\right)$$
$$= \Pr(-2.28 < Z < 0.48).$$

Now, using RESULT 2^{CRV}, we have that

$$\Pr(-2.28 < Z < 0.48) = \Pr(Z < 0.48) - \Pr(Z < -2.28).$$

We find the first part, $\Pr(Z < 0.48)$, by looking up the value in the table to get that $\Pr(Z < 0.48) = 0.6844$. For the second part, $\Pr(Z < -2.28)$, by symmetry of the normal curve, the area to the left of -2.28 is equal to the area to the right of 2.28. So, we have that

$Pr(Z < -2.28) = Pr(Z > 2.28) = 1 - 0.9887 = 0.0113$. Putting both results together, we find that $Pr(Z < 0.48) - Pr(Z < -2.28) = 0.6844 - 0.0113 = 0.6731$.

Progress Exercises

1. Suppose $X \sim N(102, 75^2)$, what is the probability that X is less than 201?

    Solution:

$$Pr(X < 201) = Pr\left(Z < \frac{201 - 102}{75}\right) = Pr(Z < 1.32) = 0.9066.$$

2. Suppose $X \sim N(50, 10^2)$, what is the probability that X is more than 60?

    Solution:

$$Pr(X > 60) = Pr\left(Z > \frac{60 - 50}{10}\right) = Pr(Z > 1) = 1 - 0.8413 = 0.1587.$$

3. Suppose $X \sim N(135, 25^2)$, what is the probability that X is less than 85?

    Solution:

$$Pr(X < 85) = Pr\left(Z < \frac{85 - 135}{25}\right) = Pr(Z < -2)$$
$$= Pr(Z > 2) = 1 - 0.9772 = 0.0228.$$

4. Suppose $X \sim N(15, 9^2)$, what is the probability that X is more than 6 and less than 19.5?

    Solution:

$$Pr(6 < X < 19.5) = Pr(-1 < Z < 0.5) = Pr(Z < 0.5)$$
$$- Pr(Z < -1) = 0.6915 - 0.1587 = 0.5328.$$

3.10 AN INTRODUCTION TO ESTIMATION*

As we mentioned at the beginning of this chapter, the objective of most statistical analysis is **inference**, that is, to estimate a parameter of a population based on sample data. Suppose, for example, that a government agency wants to estimate the average household income in Chicago. The government is likely to estimate it by sampling several "representative" households in Chicago and reporting the average of their income.

So, as we can see from this example, if we want to make an inference about a population parameter (e.g., the average household income in Chicago), we need to compute a **sample statistic** (the average income of a randomly selected sample). When a sample statistic is used to estimate a population parameter, the statistic is called an **estimator** of the parameter.

Sample statistics are computed from random variables, so they themselves are random variables and have probability distributions that are either discrete or continuous. The probability distribution of a sample statistic is called a **sampling distribution**.

3.10.1   The Sampling Distribution of the Sample Mean

Consider the problem of estimating the average monthly sales for all automobile dealers in Southern California, the mean useful life of a new lithium battery, or the average starting salary of MBA graduates. In all of these examples, we are interested in making an inference about the mean, μ, of some population.

Because many practical business applications involve estimating μ, it is important to have a sample statistic that is a good estimator of μ. The sample mean is the sample statistic used as an estimator of the population mean.

The sample mean $\overline{X}$ is a random variable whose actual value depends on the particular random sample obtained.[2] The random sample, in turn, depends on the distribution of the population from which it is drawn. As the sample size increases, however, regardless of the distribution of the population from which the random sample is drawn, the distribution of the sample mean $\overline{X}$ will be approximately normal. The result we just stated is one of the most important theoretical results in statistics and is known as the *Central Limit Theorem*.

The **Central Limit Theorem** claims that if a random sample of n observations is selected from a population with mean μ and variance σ^2, then, when n is sufficiently large, the sampling distribution of $\overline{X}$ will be approximately normal with mean μ and variance σ^2/n.

How large must the sample size, n, be so that $\overline{X}$ has a normal distribution? As a rule of thumb, we typically require $n \geq 30$ for the approximation to be valid.

Figure 3.18 illustrates the three aspects of the Central Limit Theorem with an example:

1. For *any* population distribution (even a nonnormal distribution as in panel A), when the sample size is large enough, the sampling distribution of $\overline{X}$ is normal (panel B).
2. The mean of $\overline{X}$ is μ.
3. The standard deviation of $\overline{X}$ is $\sigma/\sqrt{n}$.

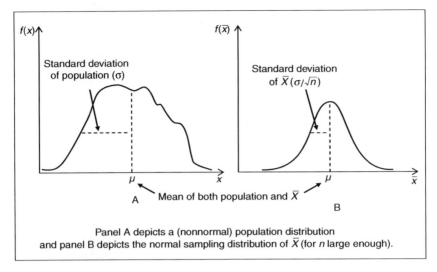

Panel A depicts a (nonnormal) population distribution and panel B depicts the normal sampling distribution of $\overline{X}$ (for n large enough).

Figure 3.18 Sampling Distribution

Example 3.10: Sampling distribution of the sample mean
A lightbulb manufacturer claims that the distribution of the lifetimes of its light bulbs has a mean of 24 months and a standard deviation of 5 months. Suppose that a consumer group decides to check this claim by purchasing a sample of 100 lightbulbs and subjecting them to tests to determine their lifetimes.

   a) Assuming that the manufacturer's claim is true, describe the sampling distribution of the mean lifetime of a sample of 100 lightbulbs.
   b) Assuming that the manufacturer's claim is true, what is the probability that the consumer's group sample has a mean lifetime $\overline{X}$ of 23 months or less?

Solution:

   a) Using the Central Limit Theorem, we know that the random variable $\overline{X}$ is approximately normal, has mean $\mu = 24$ months, and a standard deviation of $\sigma_{\overline{X}} = \frac{\sigma}{\sqrt{n}} = \frac{5}{\sqrt{100}} = \frac{5}{10} = 0.5$ month.
      So, if the manufacturer's claim is true, the sampling distribution of the mean lifetime of the 100 lightbulbs is normal with mean 24 months and standard deviation 0.5 month. The sampling distribution is shown in figure 3.19.
   b) We are looking for $\Pr(\overline{X} \leq 23)$. Since the sampling distribution is approximately normal, we can find this area by computing the z-value:

$$z = \frac{\bar{x} - \mu}{\sigma_{\bar{x}}} = \frac{23 - 24}{0.5} = -2.00$$

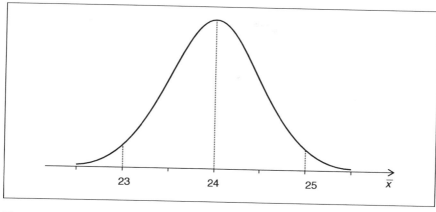

Figure 3.19 Example 3.10 Sampling Distribution

Looking in table 3.14 we find that $\Pr(Z \leq -2) = \Pr(Z \geq 2) = 1 - 0.9772 = 0.0228$. Thus, if the population mean is indeed $\mu = 24$ months and the population standard deviation $\sigma = 5$ months, the probability that the consumer group's test will result in a sample mean less than 23 months is rather small (2.3%).

3.11   REGRESSION ANALYSIS*

The major purpose of **regression analysis** is to explore the dependence of one variable on another. There are many forms of regression: linear, nonlinear, simple, multiple, and so on. Consider the simplest case: a linear regression with one predictor variable. Suppose that we have a data set that consists of n paired observations, $(x_1, y_1), \ldots, (x_n, y_n)$, and that we are interested in investigating if there is a linear relationship between x and y. A linear relationship does not mean that all the points lie exactly on a straight line, but that the points tend to cluster around a straight line.

We start by generating a scatterplot of the data. This is illustrated in panel A of figure 3.20. The n data points will not fall exactly on a straight line, but by *fitting* a line to the observed data points, as in panel B of figure 3.20, we are able to *summarize* the sample information.

3.11.1   Simple Linear Regression

A linear regression with one predictor variable is called a **simple linear regression**; as opposed to a **multiple linear regression** that deals with many predictor variables. We will concentrate exclusively on simple linear regressions since multiple linear regressions are beyond the scope of this book.

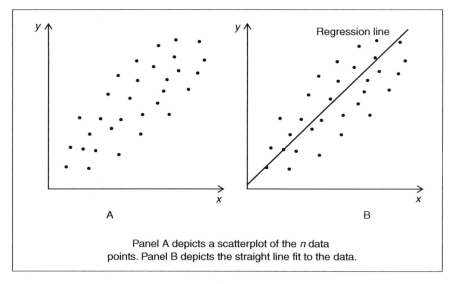

Panel A depicts a scatterplot of the *n* data
points. Panel B depicts the straight line fit to the data.

Figure 3.20 Linear Regression Analysis

In a simple linear regression, we have a relationship between x and y of the following form:

$$y_i = a + bx_i + \varepsilon_i. \tag{3.2}$$

The left-hand side of equation (3.2) is the **dependent** variable, y, which is the variable being explained by the regression. The right-hand side of equation (3.2) has two parts: the *explained* and the *unexplained* components of the dependent variable.

The **explained component** of y is $a + bx$. The quantities a and b, which represent the **intercept** and **slope** of the regression, respectively, are assumed to be fixed and unknown parameters. The variable x is the **explanatory** (or **independent**) variable. One of the main purposes of the regression is to predict y_i from the knowledge of x_i.

The **unexplained component** of y is represented by the **random error** (or **disturbance term**) ε. The random errors keep the relationship between x and y from being an exact one. If the ε_is were all equal to zero, then there would be an exact linear relationship between x and y. The effects of all factors other than variable x that influence y are included in the random error. The random error is assumed to be uncorrelated with variable x, and we also assume that $E(\varepsilon_i) = 0$.

The purpose of the regression, then, is to estimate the **regression coefficients**, a and b, of equation (3.2). That is, by running the regression, we will develop the equation that describes the relationship between x and y.

Figure 3.21 summarizes the terminology that we have introduced so far on simple linear regressions.

The estimation of the regression coefficients is based on a method called **least squares estimation**. To understand this method, consider figure 3.22. The points reflect the observed values of the dependent variable. The **fitted values** are the values of the dependent variable predicted by the regression. The **residuals** are the difference between the observed values and the fitted values.

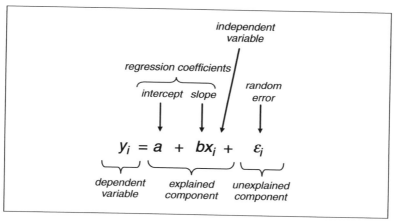

Figure 3.21   Simple Linear Regression Model

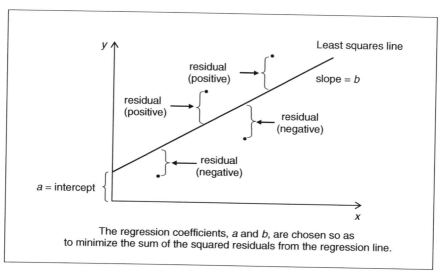

Figure 3.22   Simple Linear Regression

The **least squares line** is the line that minimizes the sum of the square residuals. Residuals are squared since, otherwise, the positive residuals would cancel out the negative residuals.

The least square line that we obtain after running the simple linear regression of equation (3.2) is:

$$\hat{y} = \hat{a} + \hat{b}x.$$

The notation " ^ " is typically used in statistics to denote a predicted value. In this case, $\hat{y}$ (read y hat) denotes predicted y. The formulas for the least square line, presented mainly for conceptual purposes (statistical software usually takes care of the calculations), are:

- The estimated intercept coefficient of the simple linear regression line, $\hat{a}$, is given by:

  $$\hat{a} = E(y_i) - \hat{b}E(x_i).$$

- The estimated slope coefficient of the simple linear regression line, $\hat{b}$, is given by:

  $$\hat{b} = \frac{Cov(y_i, x_i)}{\sigma_x^2}.$$

One way to measure the explanatory power of the regression is by the **coefficient of determination,** denoted by R^2. The coefficient of determination can be interpreted as the fraction of the variance of y explained by the regression. The formula for R^2 is given by:

$$R^2 = 1 - \frac{\sigma_\varepsilon^2}{\sigma_y^2}.$$

The value of R^2 is always between 0 and 1; the closer R^2 is to 1, the better the fit of the regression line to the observed data points.

Almost all statistical software packages perform the least square estimation method automatically. The results are typically summarized in a regression output (this is shown in example 3.11).

The regression modeling technique that we just described can be used to quantify the relationship between x (independent variable) and y (dependent variable) and to identify whether a change in x is associated with a change in y. The simple linear regression model, however, does not require the link between the two variables to be a causal link. In other words, it cannot establish whether changing x "causes" y to change.

Example 3.11: Simple linear regression
The candy shop, Candy-Candy, launched a new promotional campaign during the past month. To determine the effect of the promotional activities on sales revenue, the firm compiled a data set of the daily sales revenue and promotional expenditures.

We can define two *index* variables as follows:[3]

- Promotion: daily promotional expenditures as a percentage of day-one promotional expenditures.
- Sales: daily sales revenue as a percentage of day-one sales revenue.

Table 3.15 shows a partial listing of the data.

Data such as that in table 3.15 are called *time-series data* because it is gathered over a time sequence (days in this case). Figure 3.23 contains the scatterplot of the data on these two variables. We put the explanatory variable, promotion, on the horizontal axis and the dependent variable, sales, on the vertical axis.

The scatterplot indicates a positive relationship between promotion and sales—the points tend to rise from bottom left to top right. We can run a simple linear regression to quantify the relationship. Our objective then, is to find the least squares line for sales revenue as a function of promotional expenditure. Figure 3.24 contains the regression output (the regression was run in Microsoft Excel).

The regression output of figure 3.24 implies that the equation for the least squares line (i.e., $\hat{y} = \hat{a} + \hat{b}x$) is:

Predicted Sales $= 19.6093 + 0.6970$ Promotion.

Table 3.15 Candy-Candy Daily Promotional Expenses and Sales Revenue (Day one = 100)

Day	Promotion	Sales
1	100	100
2	86	82
3	91	92
4	74	56
5	69	59
6	90	59
7	51	54
24	102	103
25	80	90
26	62	64
27	61	74
28	76	62
29	109	99
30	70	49

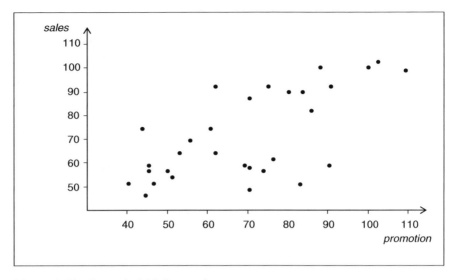

Figure 3.23 Example 3.11 Scatterplot

SUMMARY OUTPUT

Regression Statistics	
Multiple R	0.6659
R Square	0.4434
Adjusted R Square	0.4235
Standard Error	14.7020
Observations	30

These are the regression coefficients

ANOVA

	df	SS	MS	F	Significance F
Regression	1.0000	4820.9730	4820.9730	22.3040	0.0001
Residual	28.0000	6052.1405	216.1479		
Total	29.0000	10873.1134			

	Coefficients	St. Errort	Stat	P-value	Lower 95%	Upper 95%
Intercept	19.6093	10.8668	1.8045	0.0819	−2.6503	41.8689
Promotion	0.6970	0.1476	4.7227	0.0001	0.3947	0.9993

Figure 3.24 Example 3.11 Regression Output

The regression coefficient for b is 0.6970 and for a is 19.6093. The estimated slope of 0.6970 indicates that the sale index tends to increase by approximately 0.7 for every 1-unit increase in the promotion index.

The R^2 for the regression is 0.4434. This means that the variable promotional expenditure explains only 44.34% of the variation in sales revenue.

3.12 HYPOTHESIS TESTING*

Hypothesis testing is a form of decision making under uncertainty based on the choice between two competing hypothesis. The claim to be tested is called the **null hypothesis,** and it is denoted by H_0. When we set up a hypothesis test, the null hypothesis is initially assumed to be true. The **alternative hypothesis**, denoted by H_1, is the claim against the null hypothesis. The objective of hypothesis testing is to decide whether to reject the null in favor of the alternative hypothesis. Depending on the results of the test, the two possible decisions made are "reject H_0" or "do not reject H_0."

There are two types of hypotheses tests:

- **One-sided hypotheses.** In this case, the null hypothesis claims that the parameter being tested is equal to some hypothesized value and the alternative hypothesis asserts that the parameter is larger (or smaller) than that value, for example:

$$H_0 : \quad \mu = 0$$
$$H_1 : \quad \mu > 0.$$

- **Two-sided hypotheses.** In this case, the null hypothesis claims that the parameter being tested is equal to some hypothesized value and the alternative hypothesis asserts that the parameter is either larger or smaller than that value, for example:

$$H_0 : \quad \mu = 0$$
$$H_1 : \quad \mu \neq 0.$$

3.12.1 Types of Errors

In general, a hypothesis test may make one of two types of errors:

- **Type I error**: *reject* a null hypothesis that is *true.*
- **Type II error**: *do not reject* a null hypothesis that is *false.*

These two different situations are illustrated in figure 3.25. Note again that the decision made is always stated with reference to the null hypothesis.

The Type I error has been traditionally regarded as the more serious of the two errors. When setting up a test, we typically establish a desired level for the probability of a Type I error. The probability of a Type I error is called the **significance level** of the test and is denoted by α (alpha). The value of α is typically set to equal 0.01, 0.05, or 0.10. If, for example, the level of significance is $\alpha = 0.05$, then this means we will reject the null hypothesis only when the data suggest that the probability that the null is true is 5% or

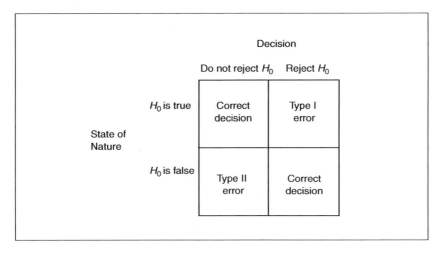

Figure 3.25 Types of Errors in Hypothesis Testing

less (i.e., the chance of making a Type I error is 5%). Studies such as clinical tests of new pharmaceutical drugs might require significance levels of 1%, while less stringent tests, such as sociological studies or business applications, might set this level at 5 or even 10%.

3.12.2 Significance from p-Values

After a hypothesis test is done, the conclusions must be reported in some statistically meaningful way. Statistically significant results are those that provide strong evidence in support of the alternative hypothesis.

One method of reporting the results of the test is to report the p-value. The **p-value** of a sample is the probability of seeing a sample with at least as much evidence in favor of the alternative hypothesis as the sample actually observed. The smaller the p-value, the more evidence there is against the null, and in favor of the alternative hypothesis. Evidence is statistically significant at the α level only if the p-value is less than α. In other words, we use the following decision rule:

Reject H_0 if p-value $< \alpha$
Do not reject H_0 if p-value $\geq \alpha$.

Example 3.12: Testing the significance of the regression coefficients
We can test the significance of the regression coefficient b of example 3.11. The hypothesis test is set as follows:

H_0: $b = 0$ The regression slope is zero, meaning that there is no (straight-line) relationship between sales and promotional expenditure.
H_1: $b > 0$ The dependent variable, sales, is sensitive (or responds) to changes in the explanatory variable, promotional expenditure.

The regression output is replicated in figure 3.26 to indicate how to look for a *p*-value.

Analyzing the regression output of figure 3.26, we find that the *p*-value of the variable promotion is **0.0001**. This number is smaller than **0.01 (1%)** so, this means we can reject the null hypothesis (no straight-line relationship between sales and promotional expenditure) in favor of the alternative at a significance level of 1%.

To better understand why we were able to favor the alternative hypothesis of a slope larger than zero for this example, let's look at figure 3.27. The

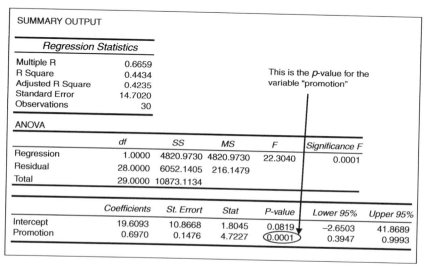

Figure 3.26 Example 3.12 Regression Output

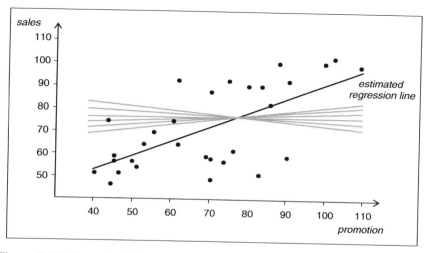

Figure 3.27 Example 3.12 Null vs. Alternative Hypothesis

light gray lines represent hypothetical regression lines in which the slope was really zero. As we can see in the scatterplot, the actual data and the estimated regression line shown in black do not conform to the pattern of the light gray lines. The hypothesis test that we just described shows this formally.

PRACTICE EXERCISES

1. Evaluate each sum.

   a) $\displaystyle\sum_{i=1}^{100} 5$

   b) $\displaystyle\sum_{i=1}^{85} 10$

   c) $\displaystyle\sum_{i=1}^{50} 1.5$

   d) $\displaystyle\sum_{i=1}^{5} 1{,}000$

2. Use the following table of values to evaluate each sum:

i	1	2	3	4	5
x_i	7	4	−2	1	3

   a) $\displaystyle\sum_{i=1}^{5} \frac{1}{5}x_i^2$

   b) $\displaystyle\sum_{i=1}^{5} 2(x_i - 1)$

   c) $\displaystyle\sum_{i=1}^{5} (2x_i - 1)$

   d) $\displaystyle\sum_{i=2}^{4} x_i^2$

3. Table 3.16 provides the daily sales of the candy shop Candy-Candy during three particular weeks. Use the information in table 3.16 to

   Table 3.16 Candy-Candy Daily Sales (Dollars, rounded to the nearest unit)

Day	Week 1	Week 2	Week 3
Monday	501	299	388
Tuesday	442	385	378
Wednesday	406	410	702
Thursday	368	134	455
Friday	492	481	470
Saturday	392	509	455
Sunday	493	477	519

calculate the mean and the median during each week. If for any week you find that the mean and the median do not coincide with each other, explain why.

4. Table 3.17 shows the frequency table of the exam score of 70 students in a Microeconomics course (the highest possible score was 100 points).

Table 3.17 Frequency Table of Exam Scores

Category	Frequency
26–40	9
41–55	13
56–70	25
71–85	15
86–100	8

a) Generate the histogram of the frequency table in table 3.17. Is there any type of skewness in the distribution of the data?

b) Assume that all scores in an interval are concentrated at the groups' midpoint. Calculate the mean, median, and mode.

5. Table 3.18 shows the frequency table of the exam score of 70 students in a Macroeconomics course (the highest possible score was 100 points).

Table 3.18 Frequency Table of Exam Scores

Category	Frequency
26–40	8
41–55	11
56–70	15
71–85	17
86–100	19

a) Generate the histogram of the frequency table in table 3.18. Is there any type of skewness in the distribution of the data?

b) Assume that all scores in an interval are concentrated at the groups' midpoint. Calculate the mean, median, and mode.

6. Table 3.19 provides the daily sales of the candy shop Candy-Candy during two particular weeks.

a) Using the information of table 3.19, calculate the mean and median daily sales for each week.

b) Calculate the sample variance and the standard deviation for each week. Interpret your results.

7. In an effort to increase sales, Candy-Candy recently started offering bonbon samples to every customer who entered the store. The owner is concerned, however, of the effectiveness of this promotional

Table 3.19 Candy-Candy Daily Sales (Dollars, rounded to the nearest unit)

Day	Week 1	Week 2
Monday	422	299
Tuesday	400	385
Wednesday	410	622
Thursday	375	134
Friday	439	481
Saturday	392	539
Sunday	432	410

Table 3.20 Candy-Candy Daily Sales and Bonbon Samples Daily Costs (Dollars, rounded to the nearest unit)

Day	Sales	Costs
1	422	33
2	400	40
3	410	42
4	375	34
5	439	31
6	392	30
7	432	40
8	523	45
9	601	48
10	366	37

practice. Table 3.20 contains a sample of 10 paired observations of Candy-Candy's daily sales and bonbon samples daily costs.

Using the information of table 3.20, calculate the sample covariance and the sample correlation coefficient between daily sales and bonbon samples daily costs. Explain your results.

8. A card is drawn out of a well-shuffled deck.
    a) What is the probability of not drawing an ace?
    b) What is the probability of drawing an even number?
9. Suppose you roll a die, let X be the number that appears on the die. Find the probability that X is larger than 2 and smaller than 5.
10. Let X be the number of defects in a machine-made product. Table 3.21 shows the probability distribution of this discrete random variable.
    a) Find the probability that the number of defects in this product is larger or equal to 2 and less than 5.
    b) Find the cumulative distribution function of this random variable.
11. Suppose that an investor has $100 worth of firm Red's stock. Let X denote the investor's payoff. Over the next month, this investment

Table 3.21 Probability Distribution of X

x	$Pr(X = x)$
0	0.1
1	0.2
2	0.2
3	0.3
4	0.1
5	0.1

could be worth:

$$x_1 = \$40, \ x_2 = \$100, \ x_3 = \$125, \text{ or } x_4 = \$150.$$

The x_i's represent the investor's payoff when event i occurs. The probabilities of each outcome are

$$Pr(x_1) = \frac{1}{4}, \ Pr(x_2) = \frac{1}{6}, \ Pr(x_3) = \frac{1}{3}, \text{ and } Pr(x_4) = \frac{1}{4}.$$

Calculate the expected value, the variance, and the standard deviation of X.

12. Suppose that an investor has $100 worth of firm Blue's stock. Let X denote the investor's payoff. Over the next month, this investment could be worth:

$$x_1 = -\$20, \ x_2 = \$90, \ x_3 = \$125, \text{ or } x_4 = \$250.$$

The x_i's represent the investor's payoff when event i occurs. The probabilities of each outcome are

$$Pr(x_1) = \frac{1}{6}, \ Pr(x_2) = \frac{1}{3}, \ Pr(x_3) = \frac{1}{3}, \text{ and } Pr(x_4) = \frac{1}{6}.$$

Calculate the expected value, the variance, and the standard deviation of X.

13. Table 3.22 contains the probability distributions of two random variables, X and Y, representing the profit from two different investments. Calculate the expected value, the variance, and the standard deviation of X and Y.

14. Candy-Candy is considering opening a second shop in Chicago. The firm has two possible location choices: Clark Street and Oak Street. Both choices are risky, since demand could turn to be either high or low. Table 3.23 shows the payoffs for each potential location.

Using the information in table 3.23, draw the firm's decision tree regarding the location. Which of the two streets is the best location?

Table 3.22 Probability Distribution of X and Y

X	$Pr(X=x)$	Y	$Pr(Y=y)$
-200	0.05	0	0.40
-100	0.10	100	0.20
100	0.10	200	0.20
200	0.25	300	0.10
500	0.50	400	0.10

Table 3.23   Candy-Candy Payoffs of Second Shop

Location	Outcome	Probability	Payoff (Dollars)
Clark Street	Demand is high	0.55	70,000
	Demand is low	0.45	25,000
Oak Street	Demand is high	0.60	100,000
	Demand is low	0.40	$-20,000$

15. Suppose that the variable X is normally distributed with a mean of 100 and a standard deviation of 20. What is the probability that X is less than 135?

16. Suppose $X \sim N(75, 6^2)$, what is the probability that X is less than 83?

17. Suppose $X \sim N(590, 55^2)$, what is the probability that X is less than 720?

18. What is the probability that a standard normal random variable z exceeds 1.75?

19. Suppose $X \sim N(590, 50^2)$, what is the probability that X is more than 619?

20. Suppose $X \sim N(160, 30^2)$, what is the probability that X is more than 100 and less than 180?

21. Suppose $X \sim N(50, 10^2)$, what is the probability that X is more than 30 and less than 60?

22. Candy-Candy conducts quality control tests on all its boxes of cookies as soon as they are out of the assembly line. The weight of the boxes is known to be normally distributed with mean $\mu = 15.5$ ounces and standard deviation $\sigma = 0.3$ ounces. Boxes must weight 15.2 ounces or more to be sold to the public. What proportion of all boxes out of the assembly line passes the quality control test?

23. The owner of Candy-Candy claims that the shop's boxes of chocolates weigh 20 ounces on average with a population standard deviation of 0.5 ounces. Suppose that a consumer group decides to check this claim by purchasing a sample of 100 boxes.

SUMMARY OUTPUT

Regression Statistics	
Multiple R	0.6307
R Square	0.3978
Adjusted R Square	0.3716
Standard Error	15.3230
Observations	25

ANOVA

	df	SS	MS	F	Significance F
Regression	1.0000	3566.6221	3566.6221	15.1905	0.0007
Residual	23.0000	5400.2350	234.7928		
Total	24.0000	8966.8571			

	Coefficients	St. Errort	Stat	P-value	Lower 95%	Upper 95%
Intercept	20.0287	12.2898	1.6297	0.1168	−5.3947	45.4522
X Variable	0.6624	0.1700	3.8975	0.0007	0.3108	1.0140

Figure 3.28 Regression Output

a) Assuming that Candy-Candy owner's claim is true, describe the sampling distribution of the mean weight of a sample of 100 boxes of chocolates.

b) Assuming that Candy-Candy owner's claim is true, what is the probability that the consumer's group sample of boxes has a mean weight $\overline{X}$ of 19.9 ounces or less?

24. Suppose that a data set consists of 25 paired observations between certain variables x and y. We ran a simple linear regression (in Microsoft Excel) to quantify the relationship between the two variables and the regression output is shown in figure 3.28.

a) What is the equation for the least squares line and the coefficient of determination of this regression?

b) Would the least squares line be upward sloping or downward sloping?

25. Using the information of figure 3.28, set a hypothesis test for the significance of the slope of the regression.

CHAPTER 4

Mathematics of Finance

Two major forces that characterize the field of finance are time and risk. These forces are incorporated in the following basic principles of finance: a dollar *today* is worth more than a dollar *tomorrow*, and a *safe* dollar is better than a *risky* dollar.

Financial assets are assets that provide a monetary flow over time. Financial assets, such as stocks or bonds, allow individuals to change their pattern of consumption over time, that is, to shift their purchasing power from high-earning periods to low-earning periods during their lifetime. Financial markets also allow investors to transfer risk from people who do not want to bear it to people who are willing to bear it if they are sufficiently compensated for it.

4.1 TIME VALUE OF MONEY

Investors often need to move money from one point in time to another. Various types of financial transactions help them to do so. For example, by temporarily lending or depositing money in a bank account, an investor can move resources from the present to the future. Alternatively, by borrowing money, an investor can move resources from the future to the present.

When one investor lends money to another, the amount borrowed is known as the lender's **principal**. The borrower is obliged to repay the principal at some particular point in time, along with a compensation for holding and using the lender's money. This compensation is called the **interest**.

The **interest rate** is the amount of interest paid on a loan during a particular time period, stated as percentage of the principal. It is the rate of return promised by a borrower to a lender. For example, suppose that you deposit $100 in a bank account that pays interest of 5% per year. In this case, you (the depositor) are the lender and the bank is the borrower. Since the annual interest rate is 5%, the $100 deposit (the principal) generates interest of $5 over the course of the year, so that the final balance after one year is $105.

With these concepts in mind, we can better understand the first basic principle of finance: *a dollar today is worth more than a dollar tomorrow*. The reason is the **time value of money**, that is, the dollar today can be invested to start earning interest immediately, so that it will be worth more than a dollar tomorrow.

4.1.1 Present Value

The **present value** (**PV**) is the current value of future cash flows discounted at the appropriate discount rate. The present value of $1 to be received t periods into the future at a discount rate (interest rate) of r is:

$$PV = \$1 \times \left[\frac{1}{(1+r)^t}\right]. \tag{4.1}$$

The term in brackets in equation (4.1) is often called the **discount factor**.

Notice that the interest rate r appears in the denominator of equation (4.1), which means that the higher the interest rate, the lower the present value. Figure 4.1 depicts graphically this inverse relationship between interest rate and present value.

The fact that the present value declines as interest rate increases means that at higher interest rates, future dollars become less expensive. For example, if the annual interest rate is 10%, to reach a $1 target a year from now, you need to deposit ¢91 today. Instead, if the annual interest rate is 20%, to reach a $1 target a year from now, you only need to deposit ¢83 today. The table in figure 4.2 contains more examples of the present value of $1 t years into the future at different discount rates.

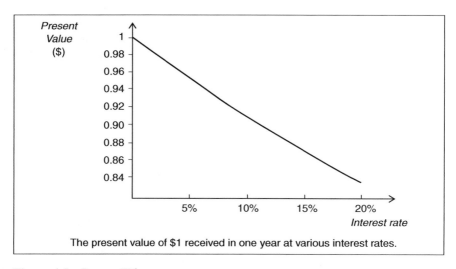

The present value of $1 received in one year at various interest rates.

Figure 4.1   Present Value

Rate	Time (t)						
(r)	1	2	5	10	15	20	25
5%	0.95	0.91	0.78	0.61	0.48	0.38	0.30
10%	0.91	0.83	0.62	0.39	0.24	0.15	0.09
15%	0.87	0.76	0.50	0.25	0.12	0.06	0.03
20%	0.83	0.69	0.40	0.16	0.06	0.03	0.01

The table contains the present value of $1 *t* years in the future
at different discount rates.

Figure 4.2 Present Value

Example 4.1: Present value

1. How much money should you invest today at a rate of 10% per year if you want to have $500 in one year?

   Solution:

   $$PV = \$500 \times \left[\frac{1}{(1+0.10)^1}\right] = \$500 \times 0.9091 = \$454.55.$$

2. How much money should you invest today at a rate of 10% per year if you want $500 in two years?

   Solution:

   $$PV = \$500 \times \left[\frac{1}{(1+0.10)^2}\right] = \$500 \times 0.8264 = \$413.20.$$

4.1.2   Future Value

The **future value** (**FV**) is the cash value of an investment at some time in the future. The future value of $1 invested for t periods at an interest rate of r per period is:

$$FV = \$1 \times (1+r)^t.$$

Example 4.2: Future value
Suppose that you invest $200 in a savings account that pays 10% per year.

a) How much money will you have in one year?
b) What would your $200 investment be worth in two years?

Solution:

a) $FV = \$200 \times (1 + 0.10)^1 = \$220$.
b) $FV = \$200 \times (1 + 0.10)^2 = \$242$.

4.2 NOMINAL AND REAL RATES OF INTEREST

The **nominal interest rate** (or nominal rate of return) is the rate at which the nominal, or dollar value, of an interest-bearing asset increases over time. The **real interest rate** (or real rate of return) on an asset is the rate at which the real value or purchasing power of the asset increases over time.

The exact relationship between the nominal interest rate r^{nom}, the real rate r, and the inflation rate denoted by π, in a given period t, is given by:

$$1 + r_t = \frac{1 + r_t^{nom}}{1 + \pi_t}. \tag{4.2}$$

If the inflation rate is not too large, the denominator in the fraction of equation (4.2) will be only slightly larger than 1. Thus, the real rate of interest can be approximated by the following expression (the symbol $\approx$ stands for approximately equal to),

$$r_t \approx r_t^{nom} - \pi_t,$$

which means that the real interest rate is approximately equal to the nominal interest rate minus the rate of inflation.

Example 4.3: Real interest rates
Suppose that the inflation rate is 2%. What is the real rate of return if the nominal interest rate is 10%?

Solution:
We calculate the real interest rate as follows:

$$1 + r = \frac{1 + 0.10}{1 + 0.02} = \frac{1.10}{1.02} = 1.078.$$

Solving for r, we get:

$$r = 1.078 - 1 = 7.8\%.$$

If we had used the approximation formula instead, we would have obtained a similar result:

$$r \approx 0.10 - 0.02 = 8.0\%.$$

4.3 COMPOUND INTEREST

If money is invested at **simple interest**, the interest is paid only on the invested amount (i.e., principal). On the other hand, if money is invested at **compound interest**, the interest earned at the end of each interest period is added to the principal, so that it too earns interest over the next period.

To illustrate the idea of compounding, suppose that you deposit $100 in an account that pays 10% per year compounded annually. Rather than withdrawing the interest, you allow it to accumulate within the account. Then:

- Your balance at the start of the first year is $100 and you finish the first year with $100 \times (1 + 0.10) = \$110$.
- Your balance at the start of the second year is $110 and you finish the second year with $110 \times (1 + 0.10) = \$100 \times (1 + 0.10)^2 = \$121$.
- Your balance at the start of the third year is $121 and you finish the third year with $121 \times (1 + 0.10) = \$100 \times (1 + 0.10)^3 = \$133.10$. And so on.

In general, the value of a principal P, invested at an annual rate of r compounded m times a year at the end of t years, is:

$$P \times \left(1 + \frac{r}{m}\right)^{m \times t}.$$

Example 4.4: Compound interest
Suppose that you invest $200 in a savings account that pays a nominal rate of 6%.

a) How much money will you have in three years if the rate is compounded quarterly?
b) How much money will you have in three years if the rate is compounded semiannually?
c) How much money will you have in three years if the rate is compounded annually?
d) How much money will you have in a year and half if the rate is compounded monthly?

Solution:

a) $\$200 \times \left(1 + \frac{0.06}{4}\right)^{3 \times 4} = 200 \times (1.015)^{12} = \$239.12$.

b) $\$200 \times \left(1 + \frac{0.06}{2}\right)^{3 \times 2} = 200 \times (1.030)^6 = \$238.81$.

c) $\$200 \times \left(1 + \frac{0.06}{1}\right)^{3 \times 1} = 200 \times (1.060)^3 = \$238.20$.

d) $\$200 \times \left(1 + \frac{0.06}{12}\right)^{1.5 \times 12} = 200 \times (1.005)^{18} = \$218.79$.

4.3.1 Continuous Compounding

The interest rate is **continuously compounded** when m, the number of times that the interest is compounded per year, is infinite. The value of a principal P, invested at a continuously compounded rate of r at the end of t years is:

$$P \times e^{rt},$$

where e is a constant and is approximately equal to 2.718.

To illustrate the impact of the number of compounding intervals on the future value of a cash flow, consider, for example, the value in five years of a $1 investment with a 10% annual rate. Figure 4.3 contains this 10% interest rate compounded at different intervals. Note that the future value increases as the number of compounding intervals increases. The reason is that interest on interest occurs sooner when there are more intervals. Thus, holding everything else constant, continuous compounding will give the largest future value.

Example 4.5: Continuous compounding
1. Suppose that you invest $100 at a continuously compounded rate of 11%.

   a) How much money will you have in one year?
   b) How much money will you have in two years?

Type of Compounding	Number of Intervals within a Year	Future Value
Annual	1	$1.6105
Semiannual	2	$1.6289
Quarterly	4	$1.6386
Monthly	12	$1.6453
Weekly	52	$1.6479
Daily	365	$1.6486
Continuous	Infinity	$1.6487

The table contains the value in 5 years of a $1 investment with a 10% interest rate and different compounding intervals.

Figure 4.3 Compounding Intervals

Solution:

a) $\$100 \times e^{0.11} = \$111.63$.
b) $\$100 \times e^{0.22} = \$124.61$.

2. What is the continuously compounded annual rate that makes a $1 investment result in $1.65 after five years?

Solution:

The information given tells us the following:

$$\$1 \times e^{5r} = \$1.65, \tag{4.3}$$

and we need to find r. Applying natural logarithms to both sides of the equation (4.3), we obtain:

$$\ln(e^{5r}) = \ln(1.65). \tag{4.4}$$

Next, we follow RULE 2ln (section 2.8.2) to calculate the left-hand side of equation (4.4). We also take the natural logarithm of the right-hand side of equation (4.4) to obtain:

$$5r = 0.5008$$
$$r = 0.1002 = 10.02\%.$$

TEST YOUR UNDERSTANDING 1

How long will it take for an investment of $500 to grow to $800 if it is invested at 6% compounded continuously?

(*Solution is in Appendix B*)

4.3.2   *Effective Interest Rate*

Suppose that a financial institution contract states that an investment will generate an annual interest of r. Let's call this the **stated interest rate**.[1] The **effective interest rate**, r_e, is the annual interest rate that is equivalent to a stated annual interest rate r compounded m times a year. The formula is given by:

$$r_e = \left(1 + \frac{r}{m}\right)^m - 1.$$

The stated interest rate is the quoted annual rate of interest uncompounded. The effective interest rate is the rate of interest actually earned. When interest is compounded more than once a year, the effective interest rate will be higher than the stated interest rate. For example, if a credit card issuer advertises an annual interest rate of 10% and this rate is compounded semiannually, the effective interest rate (what you will end up paying) is

$$r_e = \left(1 + \frac{0.10}{2}\right)^2 - 1 = 10.25\%.$$

Example 4.6: Effective interest rate

1. Suppose that an investor has to choose between two credit cards: one with a stated annual interest rate of 10% compounded daily and another with a stated annual interest rate of 10.13% compounded semiannually. Which is the better choice?

   Solution:
   Let's calculate the effective interest rate of each choice:

   $$r_e = \left(1 + \frac{0.10}{365}\right)^{365} - 1 = 10.52\%$$

   and

   $$r_e = \left(1 + \frac{0.1013}{2}\right)^2 - 1 = 10.39\%.$$

   The credit card with the higher stated interest rate (10.13%) is the better choice, since it has a lower effective interest rate.

2. Calculate the value of a $100 investment a year from now if:

   a) The stated interest rate is 10% and this interest rate is compounded quarterly.
   b) The stated interest rate is 10% and this interest rate is compounded monthly.
   c) The effective rate is 10.52%.

   Solution:

   a) $r_e = \left(1 + \frac{0.10}{4}\right)^4 - 1 = 10.38\%.$
      So, a $100 investment today would be worth $110.38 a year from now.
   b) $r_e = \left(1 + \frac{0.10}{12}\right)^{12} - 1 = 10.47\%.$
      So, a $100 investment today would be worth $110.47 a year from now.
   c) An effective interest is meaningful without the compounding interval. If we know the effective rate is 10.52%, then we can immediately tell that a $100 investment today would be worth $110.52 a year from now.

4.4 ANNUITIES

An **annuity** is an asset that pays a fixed sum each year for a specified number of years. The present value of an annuity that makes a cash payment of C from years 1 to t, given a discount rate of r, is:

$$PV \text{ annuity} = C \times \left[\frac{1}{r} - \frac{1}{r(1 + r)^t} \right].$$ (4.5)

The term in brackets in equation (4.5) is called the **annuity factor**.

Example 4.7: Annuities

1. What is the present value of an investment that offers an annual cash flow of $100 for five years if the interest rate is 8%?
   Solution:

$$PV \text{ annuity} = 100 \times \left[\frac{1}{0.08} - \frac{1}{0.08(1 + 0.08)^5} \right]$$
$$= 100 \times [12.50 - 8.51] = \$399.27.$$

2. What is the present value of an investment that offers an annual cash flow of $500 for three years if the interest rate is 10%?
   Solution:

$$PV \text{ annuity} = 500 \times \left[\frac{1}{0.10} - \frac{1}{0.10(1 + 0.10)^3} \right]$$
$$= 500 \times [10 - 7.51] = \$ 1{,}243.43.$$

4.4.1 *Amortization of Loans*

A loan is **amortized** when part of each periodic payment is used to pay the interest on the loan and part is used to reduce the outstanding principal. Since the loan is progressively paid off, the fraction of each payment devoted to interest repayments decreases steadily over time, while the fraction used to reduce the loan increases.[2]

The periodic payment is calculated by dividing the principal amount of the loan by the annuity factor. For a loan that has a principal of P and an interest rate of r, the periodic payment, C, that will be made for t periods to pay it off is calculated using the following formula:

$$C = \frac{P}{\frac{1}{r} - \frac{1}{r(1+r)^t}}.$$

Table 4.1 Amortization Schedule (Dollars)

Year	Principal Outstanding at Beginning of Period	Interest per Period	Periodic Payment	Amortization of Loan	Principal Outstanding at End of Period
		$20,000 \times 0.10 =$		$5,275.95 - 2,000 =$	$20,000 - 3,275.95 =$
1	20,000.00	2,000.00	5,275.95	3,275.95	16,724.05
2	16,724.05	1,672.41	5,275.95	3,603.54	13,120.51
3	13,120.51	1,312.05	5,275.95	3,963.90	9,156.61
4	9,156.61	915.66	5,275.95	4,360.29	4,796.32
5	4,796.32	479.63	5,275.95	4,796.32	0.00

An **amortization schedule** is a table that contains the analysis of how each payment in the loan is handled. The total interest paid is typically called the **finance charge**.

Example 4.8: Amortizing loan
Suppose that you borrow $20,000 at an interest rate of 10%. You are required to repay the loan in equal annual installments over the next five years. Compute the amortization schedule for this loan. What is the finance charge of the loan?

Solution:

To get the annual payment, we use the annuity formula as follows:

$$C = \frac{20,000}{\dfrac{1}{0.10} - \dfrac{1}{0.10(1 + 0.10)^5}} = \$5,275.95.$$

Table 4.1 contains the amortization schedule for this loan.
    The finance charge is the sum of the interest per period and is equal to $6,379.75.

4.5 PERPETUITIES

A **perpetuity** is an asset that pays a fixed sum each year forever. The present value of a perpetuity, given a discount rate of r and a cash payment of C, is calculated as follows:

$$\text{PV perpetuity} = \frac{C}{r}. \tag{4.6}$$

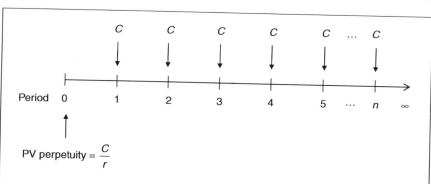

An asset that pays a fixed sum, C, each year forever.

Figure 4.4 Perpetuity

The present value formula in equation (4.6) requires that the perpetuity cash flows start the following period (i.e., at $t = 1$). Figure 4.4 illustrates the timing of the cash flows.[3]

Example 4.9: Perpetuities

1. What is the present value of an investment that offers a perpetual annual cash flow of $100 if the interest rate is 6%?

Solution:

$$PV \text{ perpetuity} = \frac{100}{0.06} = \$1,666.67.$$

2. What is the present value of an investment that offers a perpetual annual cash flow of $100 if the interest rate is 10% and the first payment will be received in five years?

Solution:

Let's first draw a time line of the situation:

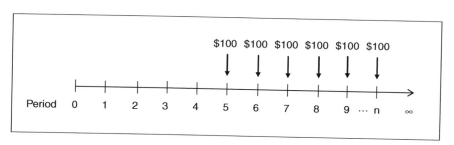

Now, let's calculate the present value of the perpetuity as of period 4. At period 4, the present value is:

$$\text{PV perpetuity} = \frac{100}{0.10} = \$1,000.$$

Since the perpetuity is worth $1,000 at period 4, we can view this perpetuity as a lump sum of $1,000 received at period 4.[4] Now, we simply need to use the present value formula discussed in section 4.1.1 to find the present value of this $1,000 lump sum:

$$\text{PV} = \$1,000 \times \left[\frac{1}{(1+0.10)^4} \right] = \$683.01.$$

TEST YOUR UNDERSTANDING 2

(1) How are annuities and perpetuities different?
(2) Suppose that you will receive an annual payment of $100 for the next 4 years (i.e., the first payment is at $t = 1$). Assume the interest rate is 10%. Calculate the present value of this annuity, using only the perpetuity formula of equation (4.6). Then, verify your results using the annuity formula of equation (4.5).

(*Solutions are in Appendix B*)

4.5.1 Growing Perpetuities

A **growing perpetuity** is an asset that pays a sum every year forever. This sum, however, is not fixed, but grows at a certain rate each year. The present value of a growing perpetuity, given a discount rate of r, a cash payment of C, and a growth rate of g (assuming $r > g$) is given by the formula:

$$\text{PV growing perpetuity} = \frac{C}{r-g}.$$

Note that a positive growth rate g reduces the denominator in the formula, resulting in a larger present value than that of the perpetuity in equation (4.6). The growth rate g can be negative in the case of a decaying cash flow.

Example 4.10: Growing perpetuities

1. What is the present value of an investment that offers a perpetual annual cash flow of $100 if the interest rate is 6% and the annual cash flow grows at a rate of 3%?

Solution:

$$PV \text{ growing perpetuity} = \frac{100}{0.06 - 0.03} = \frac{100}{0.03} = \$3,333.33.$$

2. Suppose you have an asset that generates an annual cash flow of $100, but depreciates 10% per year. What is the value of the asset if the discount rate is 5%?

Solution:

$$PV \text{ growing perpetuity} = \frac{100}{0.05 - (-0.1)} = \frac{100}{0.05 + 0.1} = \frac{100}{0.15} = \$666.67.$$

4.6 NET PRESENT VALUE

The **net present value (NPV)** of a project is calculated as the present value minus the project's required investment. Suppose that a project requires an initial investment of C_0 at time 0 (i.e., a cash outflow) and at time 1 it generates a cash inflow of C_1. The formula for calculating the NPV can be written as:

$$NPV = -C_0 + \frac{C_1}{1 + r}.$$

The appropriate discount rate, r, is the rate of return offered by equivalent investment alternatives in the capital market.

The **net present value rule** is to *accept only projects that have a positive NPV*. This rule entails accepting only those projects that are worth more than they cost and that therefore, make a *net* contribution to the investor's wealth.

Example 4.11: Net present value
You are offered a project that requires an initial investment of $500 today and generates a cash flow of $600 a year from now. Assume that common stocks with the same risk as this investment offer a 10% expected return.

a) Should you accept the project?
b) How would your answer change if the opportunity cost of capital were 25%?

Solution:

a) $NPV = -500 + \dfrac{600}{1 + 0.10} = -500 + 545.45 = \$45.45.$
Yes, you should accept the project, since it generates a cash inflow of $545.45 (in present value) and requires a cash outflow of only $500. Thus, the project increases your wealth by $45.45.

b) $\text{NPV} = -500 + \dfrac{600}{1 + 0.25} = -500 + 480 = -\$20.$

You should now reject the project because the NPV is negative (the project costs more than it is worth).

4.6.1 Discounted Cash Flow

Suppose that a project generates a series of expected cash flows from time 1 until time t. To find the present value of this project, we can add the extended stream of cash flows using the **discounted cash flow** (or **DCF**) formula:

$$\text{PV} = \frac{C_1}{1 + r_1} + \frac{C_2}{(1 + r_2)^2} + \frac{C_3}{(1 + r_3)^3} + \cdots + \frac{C_t}{(1 + r_t)^t}.$$

If such a project requires an initial investment of C_0 at time 0, then the formula for calculating the NPV can be written as:

$$\text{NPV} = -C_0 + \frac{C_1}{1 + r_1} + \frac{C_2}{(1 + r_2)^2} + \frac{C_3}{(1 + r_3)^3} + \cdots + \frac{C_t}{(1 + r_t)^t}.$$

The timeline of figure 4.5 illustrates these cash flows.

Example 4.12: NPV and DCF

1. You are offered a project that requires an initial investment of $500 today and generates the following cash flows: $200 at time 1, $150 at time 2, and $300 at time 3. The interest rate is 5%. Should you accept the project?

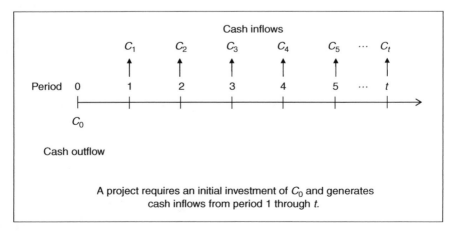

Figure 4.5 Discounted Cash Flow

Solution:

$$NPV = -500 + \frac{200}{1.05} + \frac{150}{(1.05)^2} + \frac{300}{(1.05)^3}$$
$$= -500 + 190.48 + 136.05 + 259.15 = \$85.68.$$

Yes, you should accept the project because the NPV is positive.

2. A manager is contemplating the purchase of a new machine that will cost $200,000 and has a useful life of four years. The machine would yield (year-end) cost reductions of $45,000 in year 1, $55,000 in year 2, $65,000 in year 3, and $75,000 in year 4. If the interest rate is 9%, should the manager buy the machine?

Solution:

$$NPV = -200,000 + \frac{45,000}{1.09} + \frac{55,000}{(1.09)^2} + \frac{65,000}{(1.09)^3} + \frac{75,000}{(1.09)^4}$$
$$= -\$9,099.38$$

No, the manager should not buy the machine since the NPV is negative.

4.6.2 Risk-Adjusted Discount Rates

A second basic principle of finance is that a *safe dollar is worth more than a risky dollar*. Investors undertaking higher-risk projects should be compensated with a higher expected return.

The simplest way to characterize risk is: a riskier security is one with higher **variance** (or higher **standard deviation**). To compensate investors for holding a riskier security, that security must have a higher **mean** (or **expected return**).

Once we allow for the possibility of risk, we should make two adjustments to the DCF analysis. First, we must use a **risk-adjusted discount rate**, that is, a discount rate that corresponds to the risk inherent in the project's cash flows. Let r_f be the risk-free rate on government bonds, the risk-adjusted discount rate for project i, r_i, is given by the following equation:

$$r_i = r_f + \text{Risk Premium}_i. \tag{4.7}$$

Section 4.9.3 below explains how to measure the risk of an asset and how to calculate the value of the risk premium term of equation (4.7).

The second adjustment is that, since the cash flows are uncertain, we must discount *expected* cash flows. An **expected cash flow** is a weighted average of the anticipated cash flows using the probabilities as the weights.[5]

Example 4.13: Adjusting DCF for risk
You are offered a project that requires an initial investment of $500 today, and
generates cash flows for the next two years of either $200 or $600, with equal
probability. Suppose that the discount rate for equivalent risk investments
is 20%.

a) Should you accept the project?
b) How would your answer change if the cash flows generated by the
project for the next two years were $0, $200, or $600, with equal
probability?

Solution:

a) First, let's calculate the expected cash flow of the project. If two cash
flows are equally likely, then each occurs with a probability of 0.5. Thus,
the expected cash flow is $(0.5 \times 200) + (0.5 \times 600) = \$400$. Now, we
can calculate the NPV of this project as follows:

$$NPV = -500 + \frac{400}{1.20} + \frac{400}{(1.20)^2} = -500 + 333.33 + 277.78 = \$111.11.$$

You should accept this project since the NPV is positive.

b) Let's calculate the expected cash flow of the project now. Since the three
cash flows are equally likely, each occurs with a probability of $1/3$. Thus,
the expected cash flow is $(1/3 \times 0) + (1/3 \times 200) + (1/3 \times 600) = \$266.67$. Now, we can calculate the NPV of this project as follows:

$$NPV = -500 + \frac{266.67}{1.20} + \frac{266.67}{(1.20)^2} = -500 + 222.23 + 185.19 = -\$92.59.$$

You should not accept this project since the NPV is negative.

4.7 BONDS

A **debt security** is a claim on a specified periodic stream of income. **Bonds** are
the basic debt securities. A bond is a legally binding promise to make specific
future payments. In other words, a bond is an I.O.U. When governments or
companies borrow money on a long-term basis, they often do so by issuing
bonds.

If you own a bond, you receive a fixed set of cash payments. Each year
until the bond matures, you collect a **coupon**, which is an interest payment.
At maturity, you also get back the **face value**, which is the principal amount
of the bond. The interest rate required in the market on a bond is called the
bond's **yield to maturity**. Figure 4.6 illustrates the bond's cash flows.

Bonds cash flows have an annuity (coupons) and a lump sum component
(face value paid at maturity). We can calculate the value of the bond by adding

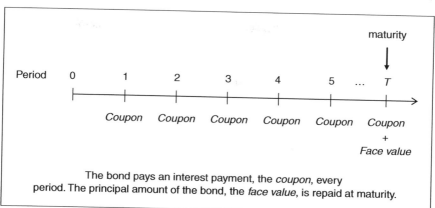

Figure 4.6 Bond's Cash Flows

the present value of these components. First, note that if a bond has a face value of F and a coupon rate of c, the coupon C is simply calculated as $C = c \times F$. Thus, the value of a bond with face value F, a coupon of C, t periods to maturity, and a yield of r per period, is given by:

$$\text{Bond value} = C \times \left[\frac{1}{r} - \frac{1}{r(1+r)^t} \right] + \frac{F}{(1+r)^t}.$$

Bonds where $c = r$ are said to be at **par**; corporate bonds are typically issued at par value. When $c > r$ the bond is at a **premium**, and when $c < r$ the bond is at a **discount**.

An important general rule in bond valuation is that there is an inverse relationship between bond prices and market interest rates. What accounts for this pattern? Unlike a bank account, a bond contract typically describes future payments in dollar amounts rather than as interest rates. When interest rates rise, the present value of the bond's future payments declines (since this is obtained by discounting at a higher interest rate). Since the promised payments are worth less in current dollars, the bond's price falls.

Let's look at the example of figure 4.7. The graph shows the price of an 8% coupon, 10-year maturity bond with face value of $1,000 for a range of interest rates. The negative slope illustrates the inverse relationship between bond prices and interest rates.

Example 4.14: Bonds
Suppose that a company were to issue a bond with 7 years to maturity, a face value of $1,000, a *semiannual* coupon of $70 (bonds issued in the United States usually make coupon payments twice a year), and a yield to maturity of 16%. What would this bond sell for?

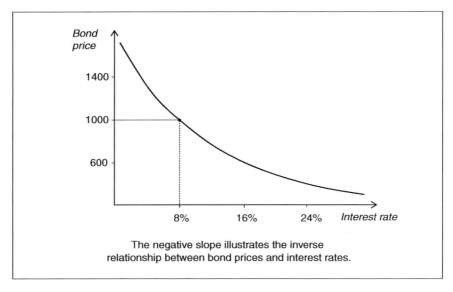

The negative slope illustrates the inverse
relationship between bond prices and interest rates.

Figure 4.7   Bond Prices and Interest Rates

Solution:

First, note that the quoted yield of 16% is an annual rate, and the coupons are
paid semiannually, so the yield over six months is 8% (that is, $\frac{16}{2} = 8$). Also,
note that during a seven-year period, there are 14 six-month periods (that is,
$\frac{12}{6} \times 7 = 14$). So, plugging in the formula we have that

$$\text{Bond value} = 70 \times \left[\frac{1}{0.08} - \frac{1}{0.08(1 + 0.08)^{14}} \right] + \frac{1,000}{(1 + 0.08)^{14}}$$

$$= 577.10 + 340.46 = \$917.56.$$

4.7.1   Zero–Coupon Bonds

A **zero-coupon bond** makes no coupon payments. In this case, investors
receive the bond's face value at maturity, but no interest payments are made
until that date (i.e., the coupon rate is zero). U.S. Treasury bills (or T-bills)
are examples of short-term zero-coupon bonds.

Zero-coupon bonds are issued at a deep discount, which means they are
initially priced considerably below face value. The investor's return comes
from the difference between the issue price and the payment of face value at
maturity. The value of a zero-coupon bond with face value F, t periods to
maturity, and a yield of r per period, is given by:

$$\text{Bond value} = \frac{F}{(1 + r)^t}.$$

Example 4.15: Zero-coupon bonds

Suppose that a five-year zero-coupon bond with face value of $1,000 has an initial price of $495. Calculate the bond's yield to maturity and the total interest paid by this bond.

Solution:

Plugging the information given to us in the bond value formula, we get that:

$$495 = \frac{1000}{(1+r)^5}. \tag{4.8}$$

Now, solving for r from equation (4.8), we get that the bond's yield to maturity is $r = 15.1\%$. The total interest paid over the life of the bond is $\$1,000 - 495 = \$505$.

4.8 COMMON STOCKS

Common stocks represent ownership shares in a corporation. Common shareholders are **residual claimants** to the assets of the firm (they are last in line of all those who have a claim on the firm's assets and income), and they have **limited liability** on their investment (the most that they can lose in the event of failure of the firm is their original investment). Shareholders generally receive **dividends** at the discretion of the board of directors.

The value of a stock is equal to the present value of all its expected future dividends. Suppose that the firm's expected dividends are forecasted to grow at a constant rate g in perpetuity. Since common stocks do not expire, we can use the present value formula for a growing perpetuity (section 4.5) to calculate the price of the stock. Let r denote the required return demanded by investors for holding the stock ($r > g$), P_0 denote the stock price today, and DIV_1 the dividend at time 1. According to the **constant-growth** (or **Gordon model**) formula, the price of the stock is given by:

$$P_0 = \frac{DIV_1}{r - g}.$$

Example 4.16: Common stocks

1. Suppose that firm Green stock is expected to pay a dividend of $6 next year. Thereafter, dividend growth is expected to be 3% forever. If the appropriate discount rate is 10 %, what is the price of the stock of firm Green today?

Solution:

$$P_0 = \frac{6}{0.10 - 0.03} = \$85.71.$$

2. You just bought a stock for $75. The stock will pay you a dividend next year and the dividend growth is expected to be 2% forever. If the appropriate discount rate is 8%, how much will you receive as dividend?

Solution:

Plugging the information in the constant growth formula, we have

$$75 = \frac{DIV_1}{0.08 - 0.02}.$$

Solving for DIV_1, we find that the dividend next year will be $4.5.

4.9 PORTFOLIO THEORY PRIMER*

A **portfolio** is a collection of assets owned by an investor. The **portfolio weights** or **proportions** are the fractions of the total portfolio value represented by each asset. The portfolio weights must sum up to one.

Investors care about the return of the portfolio as a whole, rather than the return of individual assets. As we will see next, by combining two or more assets in a portfolio, an investor can obtain a more favorable risk-return tradeoff than what any asset provides in isolation.

4.9.1 Portfolio Math

To review the basic rules of portfolio math, let's consider a particular example with two risky assets, stock M and stock H. The value of these stocks is sensitive to the state of the economy. Table 4.2 summarizes the relevant information.

The following are the basic rules governing risky assets and portfolios (p is for portfolio):

RULE 1p. The **expected return** of stock i, $E(r_i)$, is the weighted average of its returns in all scenarios, using the probabilities as weights. Denoting

Table 4.2 Rate of Return Stocks M and H (Percentage)

State of Economy	Probability of the State of Economy	Stock M	Stock H
Recession	0.4	15.5	2
Boom	0.6	6	21

the probability of scenario s as $\Pr(s)$ and the return in scenario s as $r(s)$, we have that

$$E(r_i) = \sum_{s=1}^{n} \Pr(s)r(s).$$

Using this formula to calculate the expected returns of stocks M and H, we find

$$E(r_M) = (0.4 \times 15.5) + (0.6 \times 6) = 9.8\%$$
$$E(r_H) = (0.4 \times 2) + (0.6 \times 21) = 13.4\%.$$

RULE 2p. The **variance** of stock i's return is the expected value of the squared deviations from the expected return:

$$\sigma_i^2 = \sum_{s=1}^{n} \Pr(s)\,[r(s) - E(r_i)]^2.$$

The **standard deviation** of stock i's return, σ_i, is the square root of the variance.

Applying these formulas to the data of table 4.2 we get

$$\sigma_M^2 = [0.4 \times (15.5 - 9.8)^2] + [0.6 \times (6 - 9.8)^2] = 21.66$$
$$\sigma_H^2 = [0.4 \times (2 - 13.4)^2] + [0.6 \times (21 - 13.4)^2] = 86.64;$$

and the standard deviation of each stock's return

$$\sigma_M = \sqrt{21.66} = 4.65\%$$
$$\sigma_H = \sqrt{86.64} = 9.31\%.$$

RULE 3p. The **portfolio's expected return**, $E(r_p)$, is a weighted average of the expected returns of each asset comprising the portfolio, using the portfolio proportions as weights. Denote the proportion of stock i by ω_i, then the expected return of a portfolio with N assets is given by:

$$E(r_p) = \omega_1 E(r_1) + \omega_2 E(r_2) + \cdots + \omega_N E(r_N).$$

Continuing with our example, suppose that an investor's portfolio has a proportion of 0.5 in each asset (i.e., $\omega_M = 0.5$ and $\omega_H = 0.5$), the portfolio's expected return is

$$E(r_p) = (0.5 \times 9.8) + (0.5 \times 13.4) = 11.6\%.$$

RULE 4p. The **portfolio's variance,** σ_p^2, is *not* a simple combination of the variances of the assets in the portfolio. When two risky assets, stocks i and j, are combined into a portfolio, the portfolio variance is given by:

$$\sigma_p^2 = \omega_i^2\,\sigma_i^2 + \omega_j^2\,\sigma_j^2 + 2\omega_i\omega_j\sigma_{ij}. \tag{4.9}$$

The term σ_{ij} in equation (4.9) is the **covariance** between stocks i and j. It measures how much the returns of these two risky assets move together and is calculated as

$$\sigma_{ij} = \sum_{s=1}^{n} \Pr(s)[r_i(s) - E(r_i)][r_j(s) - E(r_j)].$$

The **portfolio's standard deviation,** σ_p, is the square root of the portfolio's variance. Applying these formulas to our example, we find that the covariance between stocks M and H is

$$\sigma_{MH} = [0.4 \times (15.5 - 9.8) \times (2 - 13.4)] + [0.6 \times (6 - 9.8)$$
$$\times (21 - 13.4)] = -43.32.$$

Therefore, the variance of a portfolio that has a proportion of 0.5 in each stock is

$$\sigma_p^2 = (0.5^2 \times 21.66) + (0.5^2 \times 86.64) + (2 \times 0.5 \times 0.5 \times -43.32) = 5.42,$$

and the corresponding standard deviation is

$$\sigma_p = \sqrt{5.42} = 2.33\%.$$

RULE 5p. Let r_f denote the return of a **risk-free asset**. Because it is risk free, $\sigma_f^2 = 0$ and $\sigma_{if} = 0$. If a risky asset, stock i, is combined with a risk-free asset, the portfolio standard deviation is equal to stock i's standard deviation, multiplied by the portfolio weight on stock i:

$$\sigma_p = \omega_i\sigma_i.$$

Suppose that our investor could also invest in a risk-free asset, T-bills, which yield a sure rate of return of 5%. Let's compute the standard deviation of a portfolio that has 50% invested in T-bills and 50% invested in stock M

$$\sigma_p = 0.5 \times 4.65 = 2.33\%.$$

Table 4.3 Rate of Return Stocks A and B (Percentage)

State of Economy	Probability of the state of Economy	Stock A	Stock B	Risk-free asset
Recession	0.4	25	3	5
Boom	0.6	−2	18	5

TEST YOUR UNDERSTANDING 3

(1) Calculate the expected return of a portfolio that has 50% invested in stock M and 50% invested in T-bills.

(2) Which is a better investment strategy, a portfolio that has half in stock M and half in stock H, or a portfolio that has half in stock M and half in T-bills?

(*Solutions are in Appendix B*)

Example 4.17 Portfolio math

Table 4.3 provides the projections on stocks A and B as well as the risk-free asset.

a) Find the expected return of stock A and of stock B.
b) Find the standard deviation of stock A and of stock B.
c) What is the expected return of a portfolio that contains equal weights of stocks A and B?
d) What is the standard deviation of such portfolio?
e) What is the expected return of a portfolio that contains 70% of stock B and 30% of the risk-free asset?
f) What is the standard deviation of such portfolio?

Solution:

a) We apply RULE 1p and get:

$$E(r_A) = (0.4 \times 25) + (0.6 \times -2) = 8.8\%$$

$$E(r_B) = (0.4 \times 3) + (0.6 \times 18) = 12\%.$$

b) We apply RULE 2p and get:

$$\sigma_A^2 = [0.4 \times (25 - 8.8)^2] + [0.6 \times (-2 - 8.8)^2] = 174.96$$

$$\sigma_B^2 = [0.4 \times (3 - 12)^2] + [0.6 \times (18 - 12)^2] = 54.$$

So, we have that the standard deviations are

$$\sigma_A = \sqrt{174.96} = 13.23\% \quad \text{and} \quad \sigma_B = \sqrt{54} = 7.35\%.$$

c) We apply RULE 3p and get:

$$E(r_p) = (0.5 \times 8.8) + (0.5 \times 12) = 10.4\%.$$

d) We apply RULE 4p to obtain the covariance between stocks A and B

$$\sigma_{AB} = [0.4 \times (25 - 8.8) \times (3 - 12)] + [0.6 \times (-2 - 8.8)$$
$$\times (18 - 12)] = -97.2.$$

Next, we calculate the variance of the portfolio

$$\sigma_p^2 = (0.5^2 \times 174.96) + (0.5^2 \times 54) + (2 \times 0.5 \times 0.5 \times -97.2) = 8.64.$$

Now, we can calculate the standard deviation of the portfolio

$$\sigma_p = \sqrt{8.64} = 2.94\%.$$

e) This follows from RULE 3p as well:

$$E(r_p) = (0.7 \times 12) + (0.3 \times 5) = 9.9\%.$$

f) Following RULE 5p we get:

$$\sigma_p = 0.70 \times 7.35 = 5.15\%.$$

4.9.2   Diversification and Portfolio Risk

The principle of **diversification** tells us that spreading an investment across many assets, whose prices do not move exactly together, eliminates some of the risk. To see this, let's look at the formula for the portfolio's variance with two risky assets (RULE 4p):

$$\sigma_p^2 = \omega_i^2 \sigma_i^2 + \omega_j^2 \sigma_j^2 + 2\omega_i\omega_j\sigma_{ij}. \tag{4.10}$$

To understand this formula more clearly, let's use the correlation coefficient instead of the covariance (since the former is an easier statistic to interpret). Denoting the correlation by ρ (rho) we have that:

$$\rho_{ij} = \frac{\sigma_{ij}}{\sigma_i\sigma_j}.$$

Substituting this term into equation (4.10), we have that an alternative way of expressing the portfolio's variance is

$$\sigma_p^2 = \omega_i^2 \, \sigma_i^2 + \omega_j^2 \, \sigma_j^2 + 2\omega_i \omega_j \sigma_i \sigma_j \rho_{ij}. \tag{4.11}$$

From equation (4.11) we can derive the following result: as long as the returns from stocks i and j are less than perfectly correlated (i.e., $\rho_{ij} < 1$), the portfolio will offer a better risk-return opportunity than any of the individual assets on its own.

Let's consider an example with two risky assets, stock A and stock B. To keep things simple, suppose that both assets have the same variance and that this is given by

$$\sigma_A^2 = \sigma_B^2 = 100.$$

This is the risk that an investor faces if she holds either asset on its own. Now, suppose that the investor decides to hold a portfolio that has an equal weight on each asset (i.e., $\omega_A = \omega_B = 0.5$). Assume that the correlation coefficient is $\rho_{AB} = 0.8$. Following the formula of equation (4.11), the variance of this portfolio is given by

$$\sigma_p^2 = (0.5^2 \times 100) + (0.5^2 \times 100) + (2 \times 0.5 \times 0.5 \times 10 \times 10 \times 0.8) = 90$$

We can see that the variance of the portfolio (90) is lower than the variance of either asset on its own (100).

Diversification is not limited to two assets only; on the contrary, the larger the number of securities included in the portfolio, the larger the reduction in volatility. A well-diversified portfolio has a sufficiently large number of assets with a small weight assigned on each asset.

A large number of securities, however, cannot ultimately eliminate risk altogether, since virtually all securities are affected by marketwide risk factors. The risk that remains even after extensive diversification is called **systematic** or **market risk**. The risk that can be eliminated by diversification is called **unsystematic** or **unique risk**. Figure 4.8 illustrates these concepts.

4.9.3 Measuring Risk

For a well-diversified portfolio, unique risk is negligible. For such portfolio, essentially, all risk is constituted by market risk. The risk of a well-diversified portfolio, therefore, depends on how sensitive it is to market movements. This sensitivity to the market is called **beta**, β.

In general, the beta of stock i, β_i, is defined as:

$$\beta_i = \frac{\sigma_{im}}{\sigma_m^2},$$

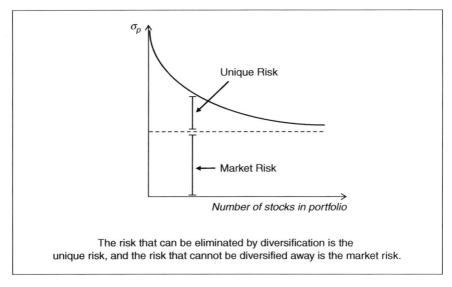

The risk that can be eliminated by diversification is the unique risk, and the risk that cannot be diversified away is the market risk.

Figure 4.8 Portfolio Diversification

where σ_{im} is the covariance between stock i's return and the market return and σ_m^2 is the variance of the market return. The return of a stock with a beta of 1 will change in exactly the same direction and magnitude as the market's return. The returns of stocks with betas greater than 1 amplify the overall movements of the market's return. The returns of stocks with betas between 0 and 1 move in the same direction as the market's return, but in a smaller magnitude.

With this information, we can determine the appropriate rate of return for stock i since, in a competitive market, this should vary in direct proportion to beta. Two assets with the same beta should have the same rate of return. This is the fundamental message of the **capital asset pricing model** (**CAPM**). The expected rate of return for any stock i is given by the following equation:

$$r_i = r_f + \beta_i(r_m - r_f), \tag{4.12}$$

where the r_f is the market risk-free rate of return, and the r_m is an estimate of the market rate of return. The term $(r_m - r_f)$ in the right-hand side of equation (4.12) is called the **market risk premium**.

As illustrated in figure 4.9, according to the CAPM model, in equilibrium, every investment should lie along a positively sloped line know as the **security market line**. Note, that if $\beta_i = 1$, then stock i has the same risk as the market, so the appropriate rate of return of stock i is $r_i = r_m$.

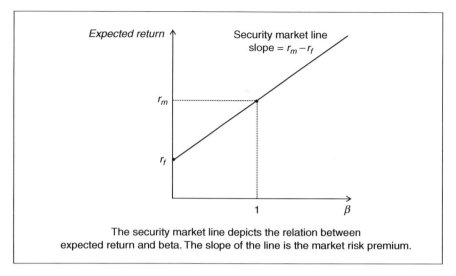

The security market line depicts the relation between expected return and beta. The slope of the line is the market risk premium.

Figure 4.9 Security Market Line

Table 4.4 Stock Z and the Market Porfolio

Variable	Value
Expected return of the market portfolio	12.1%
Market portfolio's standard deviation	0.175
Covariance between stock Z return and the market return	0.035
Risk-free rate	4.5%

TEST YOUR UNDERSTANDING 4

Suppose that the beta of stock i is equal to 0 (i.e., $\beta_i = 0$), what is the appropriate rate of return of stock i?

(*Solution is in Appendix B*)

Example 4.18: The beta of a stock

1. Table 4.4 provides information about the market portfolio.

    a) What is the beta of firm Z's stock?
    b) What is the expected return of firm Z's stock?

  Solution:

    a) $\beta_z = \dfrac{0.035}{0.175^2} = 1.14.$
    b) $r_z = 4.5 + [1.14 \times (12.1 - 4.5)] = 13.16\%.$

Table 4.5 Investment Opportunity

Variable	Value
Beta	1.5
Market risk premium	8.6%
Risk-free rate	4.5%

2. You are offered a project that costs $1,000 and has an expected cash flow in one year of $1,150. Table 4.5 provides other relevant information about this investment opportunity. Should you undertake this project?

Solution:

First let's calculate the appropriate discount rate of the project

$$r = 4.5 + (1.5 \times 8.6) = 17.4\%.$$

Now, we can calculate the net present value of the project

$$\text{NPV} = -1,000 + \frac{1,150}{(1 + 0.174)} = -1,000 + 979.56 = -\$20.44.$$

No, since the NPV is negative, you should not undertake the project.

PRACTICE EXERCISES

1. How much money must you invest today at a rate of 8% per year if you want to have $2,800 in two years?
2. How much money would you be willing to pay for an asset that generates an income of $3,000 two years from now if the interest rate is 9%?
3. Assume you deposit $1,000 today in an account that pays 4.5% interest. How much will you have in three years?
4. Assume you deposit $800 today in an account that pays 5% interest. How much will you have in five years?
5. Suppose that you are considering investing in two possible projects, A and B. Project A generates a cash flow of $1,000 in year 0 and $2,300 in year 1. Project B generates $3,400 in year 1. If the interest rate is 15%, which project is better?

6. Suppose that you are considering investing in three possible projects. Table 4.6 has the year-end profits for each option. If the interest rate is expected to be stable at 7% over the next three years, which project is best?

Table 4.6 Profits of Three Investment Opportunities

Cash Flows	Project A	Project B	Project C
Year 1	$50,000	$60,000	$70,000
Year 2	$60,000	$60,000	$60,000
Year 3	$70,000	$60,000	$50,000

7. Suppose that you invest $1,000 in a savings account that pays a nominal rate of 8% compounded quarterly. How much money will you have in a year and half?

8. Suppose that the CPI rises from 100 in one year to 105 the next. What is the real rate of return if the nominal interest rate is 12.6%?

9. Which option would you prefer?
   a. An investment that pays an interest of 13.6% compounded semi-annually.
   b. An investment that pays an interest of 13.4% compounded quarterly.
   c. An investment that pays an interest of 13.5% compounded monthly.

10. What is the value of an asset that pays a cash flow of $100 for the next 10 years if the appropriate discount rate is 5%?

11. What is the maximum that you would be willing to pay for an asset that generates $100 every year forever if the discount rate is 5%?

12. Suppose that you borrow $11,245 at an interest rate of 10%. You are required to repay the loan in equal annual installments over the next 4 years. Compute the amortization schedule for this loan.

13. What is the value of an asset that pays a cash flow of $100 in perpetuity if the appropriate discount rate is 5% and the cash flow grows at a 1% rate?

14. What is the present value of an investment that has a cash flow of $10 arriving in one year and $20 arriving in two years if the annual interest rate is 10% with semiannual compounding?

15. A manager must decide whether to purchase a machine that costs $11,000. The machine would reduce costs by $3,000 in the first year, $4,000 in the second, and $5,000 in the third year of useful life. If the interest rate is 8%, should the manager purchase the machine?

16. A project requires an initial cash outflow of $1,000. The project will produce a single cash flow two years from now, which can be either $2,100 or $100, with equal probability. If the appropriate discount rate were 8%, would you invest in this project?

17. Suppose that you need to buy a washing machine. Three stores, A, B, and C, sell exactly the same machine. Store A sells it for $600. Store B charges $625 but does not require you to make any payments for a year. Store C charges $640, but offers the following payment plan: pay $200 upfront, then $110 per year for the next four years. The interest rate is 5%. Which store offers the best deal?

18. Consider a 30-year bond a face value of $1,000 that makes a $100 coupon payment at the end of each year.
    a. Calculate the price of the bond if the interest rate is 5%.
    b. Calculate the price of the bond if the interest rate is 10%.
    c. Calculate the price of the bond if the interest rate is 15%.
    d. Based on your answers from (a)–(c), what relationship do you observe between interest rates and bond prices?

19. What is the value of a bond with 6 years to maturity, a face value of $1,000, a semiannual coupon of $50, and a yield to maturity of 12%?

20. What is the value of a 10-year bond, with face value of $1,000, a semiannual coupon of $80, and a yield to maturity of 10%?

21. What is the value of an 8% coupon, 10-year maturity bond with face value of $1,000 discounted at a semiannual rate of 5%?

22. Company Blue's stock will pay a dividend of $5 next year. The company is in a mature industry, so it expects that the dividends will increase indefinitely at a growth rate of 2% per year. If the discount rate is 8.5%, what is the price of firm Blue's stock?

23. Using the information in table 4.7, compute the expected return, the variance, and the standard deviation of a portfolio that contains 70% of stock K and 30% of stock Q.

Table 4.7 Rate of Return Stocks K and Q (Percentage)

State of Economy	Probability of the State of Economy	Stock K	Stock Q
Recession	0.5	7	10.5
Boom	0.5	18	3.5

24. Using the information in table 4.8, compute the expected return and the standard deviation of a portfolio that contains 60% of stock M and 40% of the risk-free asset.

Table 4.8 Rate of Return of Stock M
(Percentage)

State of Economy	Probability of the State of Economy	Stock K	Stock Q
Recession	0.45	3	5.5
Boom	0.55	13	5.5

25. Suppose that the risk-free rate is 4.5% and the market risk premium 7.5%. If firm Z stock has a rate of return of 15%, what is the beta of the firm's stock?

Appendix A

List of Rules

This list starts with some basic algebra rules that students might find useful when solving numerical problems. I also list all the rules covered in each chapter of the book so that this listing can be used as a reference.

Basic Algebra Rules

Negative Numbers

RULE 1. $a - (-b) = a + b$.
RULE 2. $a \times (-b) = -ab$.
RULE 3. $(-a) \times (-b) = ab$.
RULE 4. $(-a)/(-b) = a/b$.
RULE 5. $\dfrac{-a}{b} = \dfrac{a}{-b} = -\dfrac{a}{b}$.

Order of Operations

STEP 1. First, do any operations inside parentheses and do any operations involving exponents.
STEP 2. Then, working from left to right, do any multiplications or divisions in the order in which they occur.
STEP 3. Finally, working from left to right, do any additions or subtractions in the order in which they occur.

Properties of Real Numbers

Commutative Property. $a + b = b + a$.
Associative Property. Addition $(a + b) + c = a + (b + c)$.
Multiplication $(a \times b)c = a(b \times c)$.
Distributive Property. $a(b + c) = ab + ac$.

Fractions

- In the fraction $\frac{a}{b}$, a is called *numerator* and b is called the *denominator*.
- If a increases (decreases) and b is unchanged, $\frac{a}{b}$ increases (decreases).

- If b increases (decreases) and a is unchanged, $\frac{a}{b}$ decreases (increases).
- Note that $\frac{ax}{b} = \frac{a}{b}x$.

Operations with Fractions

Multiplication. $\frac{a}{b} \times \frac{c}{d} = \frac{ac}{bd}$.

Division. $\frac{a}{b} \div \frac{c}{d} = \frac{ad}{bc}$.

Addition. With common denominator $\frac{a}{b} + \frac{c}{b} = \frac{a+c}{b}$.

With no common denominator $\frac{a}{b} + \frac{c}{d} = \frac{ad+cb}{bd}$.

Polynomials

RULE 1. $(x + a)^2 = x^2 + 2ax + a^2$.
RULE 2. $(x - a)^2 = x^2 - 2ax + a^2$.
RULE 3. $(x + a)(x + b) = x^2 + (a + b)x + ab$.
RULE 4. $x^2 - a^2 = (x + a)(x - a)$.

Chapter 1   Business Math: Functions and Graphs

Solving Linear Equations

RULE 1eq. A term can be moved from one side of an equation to the other if and only if its sign is changed to the opposite sign as it crosses the equal sign.

RULE 2eq. Both sides of an equation can be multiplied or divided by the same nonzero number and the equation is unaltered.

Solving Linear Inequalities

RULE 1in. If the same number is added (or subtracted) to both sides of an inequality, the resulting inequality has the same direction as the original inequality.

RULE 2in. If both sides of an inequality are multiplied (or divided) by the same *positive* number, the resulting inequality has the same direction as the original inequality.

RULE 3in. If both sides of an inequality are multiplied (or divided) by the same *negative* number, the resulting inequality has the reverse direction of the original inequality.

Exponents

RULE 1x. $x^0 = 1$.
RULE 2x. $x^a \times x^b = x^{a+b}$.
RULE 3x. $(x^a)^b = x^{ab}$.
RULE 4x. $(xz)^a = x^a \times z^a$.
RULE 5x. $\left(\frac{x}{z}\right)^a = \frac{x^a}{z^a}$.
RULE 6x. $\frac{x^a}{x^b} = x^{a-b}$.

RULE 7x. $x^{-a} = \frac{1}{x^a}$ and $\frac{1}{x^{-a}} = x^a$.

Square Roots

RULE 1r. $\sqrt{x} \cdot \sqrt{z} = \sqrt{xz}$.
RULE 2r. $\frac{\sqrt{x}}{\sqrt{z}} = \sqrt{\frac{x}{z}}$.
RULE 3r. $\sqrt{0} = 0$.
RULE 4r. $\sqrt{x} \geq 0$.
RULE 5r. $\sqrt{x^3} = x \cdot \sqrt{x} \geq 0$.

Growth Rates

RULE 1g. % growth rate of $(xz) = \%\Delta x + \%\Delta z$.
RULE 2g. % growth rate of $\left(\frac{x}{z}\right) = \%\Delta x - \%\Delta z$.
RULE 3g. % growth rate of $(x^a) = a(\%\Delta x)$.

Chapter 2   Business Math: Optimization

Derivatives

RULE 1d. If $f(x) = c$, where c is a constant, then $f'(x) = 0$.
RULE 2d. If $f(x) = x^a$, where a is any number, then $f'(x) = ax^{a-1}$.
RULE 3d. If $f(x) = cg(x)$, where c is a constant, then $f'(x) = cg'(x)$.
RULE 4d. If $f(x) = g(x) \pm h(x)$, then $f'(x) = g'(x) \pm h'(x)$.
RULE 5d. If $f(x) = a + bx$, then $f'(x) = b$. Note, this is the equation of a line and b is the slope.
PRODUCT RULE. If $f(x) = g(x) \cdot h(x)$, then $f'(x) = [g(x) \cdot h'(x)] + [h(x) \cdot g'(x)]$.
QUOTIENT RULE. If $f(x) = \frac{g(x)}{h(x)}$, then $f'(x) = \frac{[h(x)\cdot g'(x)]-[g(x)\cdot h'(x)]}{[h(x)]^2}$.
POWER OF A FUNCTION (CHAIN RULE). If $f(x) = [g(x)]^n$, then $f'(x) = n[g(x)]^{n-1}g'(x)$.

Exponential Functions

RULE 1e. e^x is always positive.
RULE 2e. e raised to any power can never equal zero, therefore, $e^x = 0$ has no solution.
RULE 3e. $e^0 = 1$.

Common Logarithms

For $x, z > 0$:

RULE 1log. $\log(1) = 0$
RULE 2log. $\log(10) = 1$.
RULE 3log. $\log(xz) = \log(x) + \log(z)$.
RULE 4log. $\log\left(\frac{x}{z}\right) = \log(x) - \log(z)$.

RULE 5log. $\log(x^z) = z\log(x)$.

Natural Logarithm

For $x, z > 0$:

RULE 1ln. $\ln(e) = 1$.
RULE 2ln. $\ln(e^x) = x$.
RULE 3ln. $\ln(1) = 0$.
RULE 4ln. $\ln(xz) = \ln(x) + \ln(z)$.
RULE 5ln. $\ln(x^z) = z\ln(x)$.

Chapter 3   Statistical Analysis Primer

Summation

For a constant c:

RULE 1s. $\sum_{i=1}^{n} cx_i = c\sum_{i=1}^{n} x_i$.

RULE 2s. $\sum_{i=1}^{n} c = c\sum_{i=1}^{n} 1 = cn$.

Continuous Random Variable

If X is a continuous random:

RESULT 1^{CRV}. $\Pr(X > a) = 1 - \Pr(X < a)$.
RESULT 2^{CRV}. $\Pr(a < X < b) = \Pr(X < b) - \Pr(X < a)$. Assuming that $a < b$.
RESULT 3^{CRV}. $\Pr(a < X < b) = \Pr(a < X \leq b) = \Pr(a \leq X < b) = $
$\Pr(a \leq X \leq b)$.

Chapter 4   Mathematics of Finance

Portfolio Math

RULE 1p. Denote the probability of scenario s as $\Pr(s)$ and the return in scenario s as $r(s)$, the **expected return** of stock i is given by:
$$E(r_i) = \sum_{s=1}^{n} \Pr(s)r(s).$$

RULE 2p. The **variance** of stock i's return is given by: $\sigma_i^2 = \sum_{s=1}^{n} \Pr(s)\,[r(s) - E(r_i)]^2$.
The **standard deviation** of stock i's return, σ_i, is the square root of the variance.

RULE 3p. Denote the proportion of stock i by ω_i, then the **expected return of a portfolio** with N assets is given by: $E(r_p) = \omega_1 E(r_1) + \omega_2 E(r_2) + \cdots + \omega_N E(r_N)$.

RULE 4p. When two risky assets, stocks i and j, are combined into a portfolio, the **portfolio' variance** is given by: $\sigma_p^2 = \omega_i^2 \sigma_i^2 + \omega_j^2 \sigma_j^2 + 2\omega_i\omega_j\sigma_{ij}$. The term σ_{ij} is the **covariance** between stocks i and j and is calculated as $\sigma_{ij} = \sum_{s=1}^{n} \Pr(s)[r_i(s) - E(r_i)][r_j(s) - E(r_j)]$. The **portfolio's standard deviation**, σ_p, is the square root of the portfolio's variance.

RULE 5p. Let r_f denote the return of a **risk-free asset**. If a risky asset, stock i, is combined with a risk-free asset, the portfolio's standard deviation is given by: $\sigma_p = \omega_i\sigma_i$.

Appendix B

Answers to Practice Exercises

CHAPTER 1

TEST YOUR UNDERSTANDING 1

(1) $p = 1 - 2Q^d$
(2) $p = 4 - \frac{2}{3}Q^d$

TEST YOUR UNDERSTANDING 2

(1)

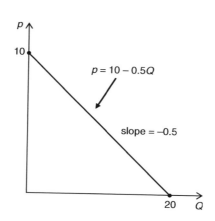

(2)

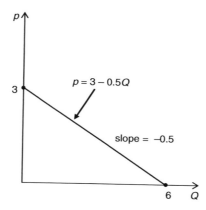

TEST YOUR UNDERSTANDING 3

(1)

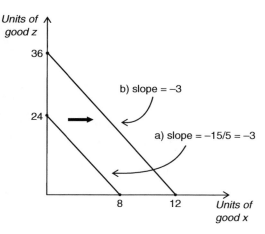

(2)

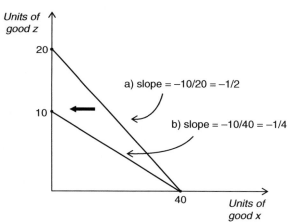

TEST YOUR UNDERSTANDING 4

(1) $p^* = 7$ and $Q^* = 19$
(2) $p^* = 5$ and $Q^* = 15$
(3) $p^* = 20$ and $Q^* = 100,000$

PRACTICE EXERCISES

1. $y = 12 - x$
2. $y = 3 - 3x$
3. $y = 2x + 30$
4. $x^* = 5$
5. $x^* = 6$

6.

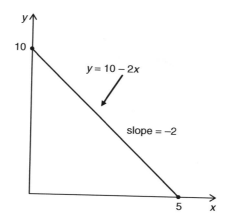

7.

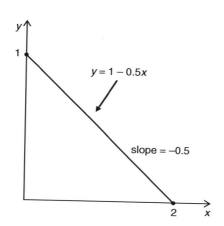

8.

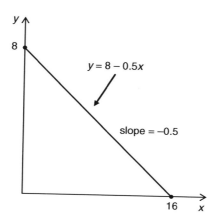

9.

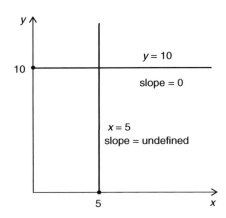

10.

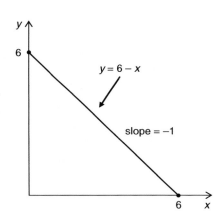

11. $x^* = 5$ and $y^* = 25$
12. $x^* = 4$ and $y^* = 6$
13. $x^* = 2$ and $y^* = 1$
14.

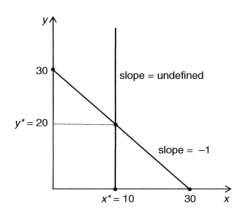

15.

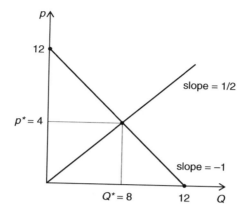

16.

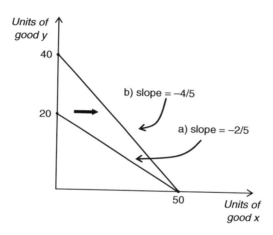

17.

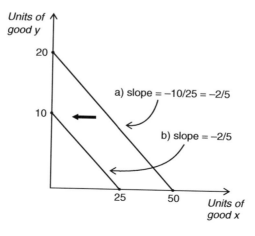

18.

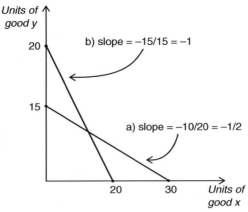

19. We know that at equilibrium, supply and demand are equal. So, we have that at equilibrium

$$30 - 2p = 4p.$$

Then, we solve for equilibrium price and find that $p^* = 5$. Now, we substitute this price into either the demand or the supply to find the equilibrium quantity, $Q^* = 30 - 2(5) = 20$.

20. We know that at equilibrium, supply and demand are equal. So, we have that at equilibrium

$$20 - p = 5 + 2p.$$

Then, we solve for equilibrium price and find that $p^* = 5$. Now, we substitute this price into either the demand or the supply to find the equilibrium quantity, $Q^* = 20 - 5 = 15$.

21. With $p_{wine} = 20$ and $I = 10$, the demand for beer becomes: $Q^d_{beer} = 200 - 4p_{beer}$. At equilibrium, supply and demand are equal so we have that

$$200 - 4p_{beer} = 100 + 6p_{beer}.$$

Next, we solve for the equilibrium price and find that $p^*_{beer} = 10$. Finally, substitute this price into either the demand or the supply to find that the corresponding quantity is $Q^*_{beer} = 100 + 6(10) = 160$.

22.

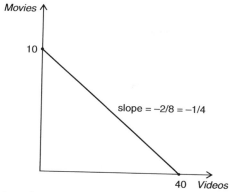

23. With $p_f = 10$ and $p_c = 4$, the demand and supply relationships become

$$Q_b^s = 20 + 2p,$$
$$Q_b^d = 68 - 10p_b.$$

To get the equilibrium price, we set demand and supply equal to each other,

$$20 + 2p_b = 68 - 10p_b$$

and solve for price to get $p_b^* = 4$. Then, we substitute this price into either the demand or the supply to find an equilibrium quantity of $Q_b^* = 28$.

24. Substituting the values given we have $\%\Delta Y = (0.3 \times 2\%) + (0.7 \times 3\%) = 2.7\%$.

25. Substituting the values given we have $3.4\% = (0.3 \times 2\%) + 0.7(\%\Delta L)$, so solving for the growth rate of labor, $\%\Delta L$, we find that $\%\Delta L = 4\%$.

CHAPTER 2

TEST YOUR UNDERSTANDING 1

(1) $MC(q) = C'(q) = 5$
(2) $MC(q) = C'(q) = 4q$

TEST YOUR UNDERSTANDING 2

a. The firm is able to produce $q(4) = 12(4)^{0.5} = 24$ units of output.

b. To get this, we calculate the derivative of the function

$$MPL = q'(L) = 12(0.5)L^{-0.5} = \frac{6}{\sqrt{L}}$$

and evaluate it at $L = 4$ to get $MPL = q'(4) = \frac{6}{\sqrt{4}} = 3$.

   c. Our result from part (b) suggests that, with the existing labor
     force, hiring an additional worker would increase output by 3
     units.

TEST YOUR UNDERSTANDING 3

First, we get the FOC: $\Pi'(q^*) = 1,000 - 10q^* = 0$. Solving this FOC gives
us $q^* = 100$. Finally, we verify that this value is a maximum with the SOC:
$\Pi''(q^*) = -10 < 0$.

   At this level of output, the firm makes profits of $\Pi(100) = 1,000(100) - 5(100^2) = \$50,000$.

TEST YOUR UNDERSTANDING 4

Table A.1 Data for Calculation of Output With Base
Year = Year 2

	Current Quantities	Base Year Prices
Year 1		
Surfboards	100	$250/board
Computers	2	$500/computer
Year 2		
Surfboards	120	$250/board
Computers	6	$500/computer

Real GDP in year 2 is \$33,000 (in the base year, nominal GDP = real GDP)
and real GDP in year 1 is $GDP_1 = (100 \times \$250) + (2 \times \$500) = \$26,000$.
So, we have that output, as measured by real GDP, is 26.9% higher in year 2
than in year 1.

PRACTICE EXERCISES

1. $f'(x) = 8x - 5$.
2. $f'(x) = 10x - 12x^2 + 1$.
3. $f'(x) = \frac{1}{2}x^{-\frac{1}{2}} = \frac{1}{2} \cdot \frac{1}{\sqrt{x}}$.
4. $f'(x) = 8x - 3x^2 + 2$.
5. $f'(x) = -33 + x$.
6. First, we find the derivative of the function

$$f'(x) = 2x.$$

Then, we evaluate it at $x = 3$,

$f'(3) = 2 \cdot 3 = 6.$

So, the slope of the line tangent to the function at $x = 3$ is 6.
7. First, we find the derivative of the function

$$f'(x) = 2\left(\frac{1}{2}x^{-\frac{1}{2}}\right) = \frac{1}{\sqrt{x}}.$$

Then, we evaluate it at $x = 9$,

$$f'(9) = \frac{1}{\sqrt{9}} = \frac{1}{3}.$$

So, the slope of the line tangent to the function at $x = 9$ is $\frac{1}{3}$.
8. $f'(x) = 2x + 3$ and $f''(x) = 2.$
9. $f'(x) = 12x^2 - 6x$, and $f''(x) = 24x - 6.$
10. It is a convex function, since its second derivative is positive: $f'(x) = 2x$ and $f''(x) = 2 > 0.$
11. It is a concave function, since its second derivative is negative: $f'(x) = \frac{1}{2}x^{-\frac{1}{2}}$ and $f''(x) = -\frac{1}{4}x^{-\frac{3}{2}} < 0.$
12. $\frac{\partial f}{\partial x} = 16x - 5z$ and $\frac{\partial f}{\partial z} = -5x.$
13. $\frac{\partial Q}{\partial L} = 0.5K^{0.5}L^{-0.5} = 0.5\frac{K^{0.5}}{L^{0.5}}$ and $\frac{\partial Q}{\partial K} = 0.5L^{0.5}K^{-0.5} = 0.5\frac{L^{0.5}}{K^{0.5}}.$
14. $\frac{\partial f}{\partial p} = -1$, $\frac{\partial f}{\partial I} = -30$, and $\frac{\partial f}{\partial m} = 55.$
15. FOC: $\Pi'(q^*) = 50 - 2q^* = 0$, solving for q^* we get that $q^* = 25.$
    Next, we verify that with the SOC that this value is indeed a maximum (we need to show that the second derivative is negative).

SOC: $\Pi''(q^*) = -2 < 0.$

Since both the FOC and SOC hold, we can be sure this is a maximum.
16. FOC: $C'(q) = 8q^* - 16 = 0$, solving for q^* we get that $q^* = 2.$
    Next, we verify that with the SOC that this value is indeed a minimum (we need to show that the second derivative is positive).

SOC: $C''(q) = 8 > 0.$

Since both the FOC and SOC hold, we can be sure this is a minimum.

17.

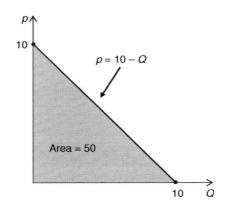

18.

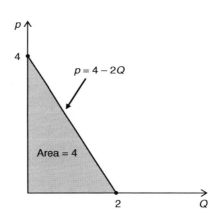

19.

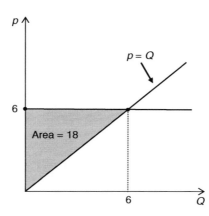

20.

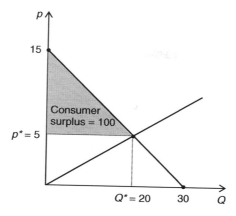

21.

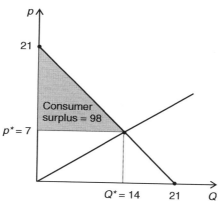

22. FOC: $C'(q^*) = 4q^* - 36 = 0$, solving for q^* we get that $q^* = 9$.
Next, we verify that with the SOC that this value is indeed a minimum (we need to show that the second derivative is positive).

SOC: $C''(q^*) = 4 > 0$.

Since both the FOC and SOC hold, we can be sure $q^* = 9$ minimizes the function.

23. To find the value q^* at which the function is minimized, we get the FOC, by taking the derivative of the function and setting it equal to zero.

FOC: $C'(q^*) = 6q^* - 120 = 0$.

Solving for q^* we get $q^* = 20$ units.

We now verify, through the SOC, that $q^* = 20$ is indeed a minimum.

SOC: $C''(q^*) = 6 > 0$.

Since both the FOC and SOC hold, we can be sure $q^* = 20$ minimizes the function.

At this level of output, costs are equal to $C(20) = (3 \times 20^2) - (120 \times 20) + 1,750 = \$550$.

24. To find the value q^* at which the function is maximized, we get the FOC, by taking the derivative of the function and setting it equal to zero.

FOC: $\Pi'(q^*) = 16 - 2q^* = 0$.

Solving for q^* we get $q^* = 8$.

We now verify, through the SOC, that $q^* = 8$ is indeed a maximum.

SOC: $\Pi''(q^*) = -2 < 0$.

The second derivative is smaller than zero. Since both the FOC and SOC hold, we can conclude that the level of output that maximizes profits for this firm is $q^* = 8$.

At this level of output, profits are equal to $\Pi(8) = (16 \times 8) - 10 - 8^2 = \$54$.

25. FOC: $\Pi'(q^*) = 8 - q^* = 0$.

Solving for q^* we get $q^* = 8$.

Now verify, through the SOC, that $q^* = 8$ is indeed a maximum.

SOC: $\Pi''(q^*) = -1 < 0$.

Since both the FOC and SOC hold, we can conclude that the level of output that maximizes profits for this firm is $q^* = 8$.

At this level of output, profits are equal to $\Pi(8) = 8(8) - \frac{1}{2}(8)^2 - 2 = \$30$.

CHAPTER 3

TEST YOUR UNDERSTANDING 1

(1) The smallest possible value of the variance is zero.
(2) The units of the variance are squared units of the original data.

TEST YOUR UNDERSTANDING 2

(1) No, if $r_{xy} = 0$, it means that there is no *linear* relationship between x and y.
(2) The covariance between a variable and itself is the *variance* of that variable.

PRACTICE EXERCISES

1. a) $\sum_{i=1}^{100} 5 = 5 \sum_{i=1}^{100} 1 = 5 \times 100 = 500.$

    b) $\sum_{i=1}^{85} 10 = 10 \times 85 = 850.$

    c) $\sum_{i=1}^{50} 1.5 = 1.5 \times 50 = 75.$

    d) $\sum_{i=1}^{5} 1,000 = 1,000 \times 5 = 5,000.$

2. a) $\frac{1}{5} \sum_{i=1}^{5} x_i^2 = \frac{1}{5} \times 79 = 15.8.$

    b) $2 \sum_{i=1}^{5} (x_i - 1) = 2 \times 8 = 16.$

    c) $\sum_{i=1}^{5} (2x_i - 1) = 21.$

    d) $\sum_{i=2}^{4} x_i^2 = 21.$

3. The results are summarized in table A.2 below:

Table A.2 Mean and Median Weekly Sales (Dollars)

	Week 1	Week 2	Week 3
Mean	442	385	481
Median	442	410	455

In week 2, Thursday's sales value is relatively low, this pulls the mean down and thus, the mean is below the median. In week 3, Wednesday's relatively high value pulls the mean above the median.

4.

a)

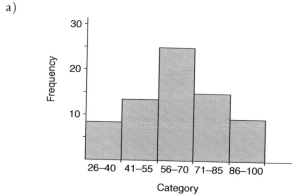

The histogram is symmetric (i.e., no skewness).

b) The mean is $\bar{x} = \frac{4,410}{70} = 63$ points. The median is the average of the 35th and 36th observations and both of these lie on the interval 56–70, so, the midpoint, 63, is the median. The mode lies on the highest bar of the histogram which is the interval 56–70, so, the midpoint, 63, is the mode as well.

5.

a)

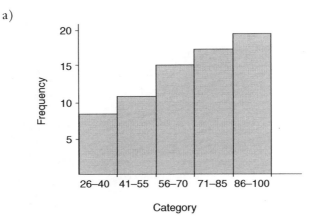

Category

The histogram is negatively skewed (i.e., skewed to the left).

b) The mean is $\bar{x} = \frac{4,830}{70} = 69$ points. The median is the average of the 35th and 36th observations and both of these lie on the interval 71–85, so, the midpoint, 78, is the median. The mode lies on the highest bar of the histogram which is the interval 86–100, so, the midpoint, 93, is the mode.

6. a) The mean for week 1 and for week 2 is $\bar{x} = \frac{2,870}{7} = \$410$. The median is also $410 for both weeks.

b) The results are summarized in table A.3 below:

Table A.3 Measures of Dispersion of Weekly Sales

	Week 1	Week 2
Variance	519.67	25,958
Standard Deviation	$22.80	$161.11

What these results tell us is that, even though sales during both weeks were centered at $410, there was more variability in the daily sales during week 2 than during week 1.

7. Let x = bonbon samples daily costs and y = daily sales. Using the sample data of table 3.20, we get the following results:

$$Cov(x, y) = \frac{\sum_{i=1}^{10}(x_i - 38)(y_i - 436)}{10 - 1} = \frac{2,790}{9} = 310$$

$$Corr(x, y) = r_{xy} = \frac{310}{6.04 \times 72.68} = 0.71.$$

What these results tell us is that bonbon samples daily costs and sales revenue are positively linearly related. Furthermore, a correlation coefficient of 0.71 indicates that the positive relationship between these two variables is strong (remember, however, that correlation does not imply causality).

8. a) $Pr(\textit{not ace}) = 1 - Pr(\textit{ace}) = 1 - \frac{4}{52} = \frac{48}{52} = \frac{12}{13}$.
    b) $Pr(\textit{even}) = \frac{20}{52} = \frac{5}{13}$.
9. $Pr(2 < X < 5) = Pr(X = 3) + Pr(X = 4) = \frac{1}{6} + \frac{1}{6} = \frac{2}{6} = \frac{1}{3}$.
10. a) $Pr(2 \leq X < 5) = Pr(X = 2) + Pr(X = 3) + Pr(X = 4) = 0.6$.
    b)

Table A.4 Cumulative Distribution Function of X

x	$Pr(X \leq x)$
0	0.1
1	0.3
2	0.5
3	0.8
4	0.9
5	1.0

11. $E(X) = \left(\frac{1}{4} \times 40\right) + \left(\frac{1}{6} \times 100\right) + \left(\frac{1}{3} \times 125\right) + \left(\frac{1}{4} \times 150\right) = \$105.83$

$$\sigma_x^2 = \left(\frac{1}{4}[40 - 105.83]^2\right) + \left(\frac{1}{6}[100 - 105.83]^2\right)$$
$$+ \left(\frac{1}{3}[125 - 105.83]^2\right) + \left(\frac{1}{4}[150 - 105.83]^2\right)$$
$$= 1,699.31$$
$$\sigma_x = \sqrt{1,699.31} = \$41.22.$$

12. $E(X) = \left(\frac{1}{6} \times -20\right) + \left(\frac{1}{3} \times 90\right) + \left(\frac{1}{3} \times 125\right) + \left(\frac{1}{6} \times 250\right) = \$110$

$$\sigma_x^2 = \left(\frac{1}{6}[-20-110]^2\right) + \left(\frac{1}{3}[90-110]^2\right) + \left(\frac{1}{3}[125-110]^2\right)$$
$$+ \left(\frac{1}{6}[250-110]^2\right) = 6,291.67$$

$$\sigma_x = \sqrt{6,291.67} = \$79.32.$$

13. $E(X) = 290$ and $E(Y) = 130$

$$\sigma_x^2 = 54,900 \quad \text{and} \quad \sigma_y^2 = 18,100$$
$$\sigma_x = 234.31 \quad \text{and} \quad \sigma_y = 134.54.$$

14.

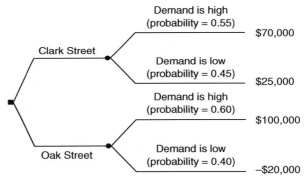

To decide which is the better location, we need to compute the expected value of each possible choice.

$E(\text{Clark Street}) = (0.55 \times \$70,000) + (0.45 \times \$25,000) = \$49,750$

$E(\text{Oak Street}) = (0.60 \times \$100,000) + (0.40 \times -20,000) = \$52,000.$

The better location is Oak Street.

15. We first standardize the value 135 to get the corresponding z-value:

$$z = \frac{135-100}{20} = 1.75.$$

We then look up the value 1.75 in table 3.14 (1.7 row, 0.05 column) and find that the probability is 0.9599.

16. We first standardize the value 83 to get the corresponding z-value:

$$z = \frac{83-75}{6} = 1.33.$$

We then look up the value 1.33 in table 3.14 (1.3 row, 0.03 column) and find that the probability is 0.9082.

17. We first standardize the value 720 to get the corresponding z-value:

$$z = \frac{720 - 590}{55} = 2.36.$$

We then look up the value 2.36 in table 3.14 (2.3 row, 0.06 column) and find that the probability is 0.9909.

18. To find the probability that z exceeds 1.75, we can first find the probability that it is less than 1.75, then we subtract this probability to 1 (remember the total area under the curve is 1). If we look up the value of 1.75 in table 3.14 (1.7 row, 0.05 column), we find that the probability z is *less* than 1.75 is 0.9599. This means, that the probability that z is *more* than 1.75 is $1 - 0.9599 = 0.0401$.

19. To find the probability that z exceeds 0.58, we can first find the probability that it is less than 0.58, then we subtract this probability to 1. If we look up the value of 0.58 in table 3.14 (0.5 row, 0.08 column), we find that the probability z is *less* than 0.58 is 0.7190. This means, that the probability that z is *more* than 0.58 is $1 - 0.7190 = 0.2810$.

20. Using the corresponding z-values we have that

$$\Pr\left(\frac{100 - 160}{30} < Z < \frac{180 - 160}{30}\right) = \Pr(-2 < Z < 0.67).$$

From RESULT 2^{CRV}, we know that

$$\Pr(-2 < Z < 0.67) = \Pr(Z < 0.67) - \Pr(Z < -2).$$

We look up in table 3.14 the value of the first part, $\Pr(Z < 0.67)$, and get that $\Pr(Z < 0.67) = 0.7486$. For the second part, $\Pr(Z < -2)$, we know that, by symmetry of the normal curve, the area to the left of -2 is equal to the area to the right of 2, so, we have that $\Pr(Z < -2) = \Pr(Z > 2) = 1 - 0.9772 = 0.0228$. Putting both results together, we find that $\Pr(Z < 0.67) - \Pr(Z < -2) = 0.7486 - 0.0228 = 0.7258$.

21. Using the corresponding z-values we have that

$$\Pr\left(\frac{30 - 50}{10} < Z < \frac{60 - 50}{10}\right) = \Pr(-2 < Z < 1).$$

From RESULT 2^{CRV}, we know that

$$\Pr(-2 < Z < 1) = \Pr(Z < 1) - \Pr(Z < -2).$$

We look up in table 3.14 the value for $\Pr(Z < 1)$, and get that $\Pr(Z < 1) = 0.8413$. For $\Pr(Z < -2)$, we know that, by symmetry of the normal curve, the area to the left of -2 is equal to the area to the right of 2, so, we have that $\Pr(Z < -2) = \Pr(Z > 2) = 1 - 0.9772 = 0.0228$. Putting both results together, we find that $\Pr(Z < 1) - \Pr(Z < -2) = 0.8413 - 0.0228 = 0.8185$.

22. $\Pr(X > 15.2) = \Pr(Z > \frac{15.2-15.5}{0.3}) = \Pr(Z > -1) = 0.8413$.
   Thus, 0.8413 or 84.13% of all boxes coming out of the assembly line will pass the quality control test.

23.   a) Using the Central Limit Theorem, we know that the random variable $\overline{X}$ is approximately normal, has mean $\mu = 20$ ounces, and a standard deviation of $\sigma_{\overline{X}} = \frac{\sigma}{\sqrt{n}} = \frac{0.5}{\sqrt{100}} = \frac{0.5}{10} = 0.05$ ounces. So, if Candy-Candy owner's claim is true, the sampling distribution of the mean weight of the 100 boxes of chocolates is normal with mean 20 ounces and standard deviation 0.05 ounces.

   b) We are looking for $\Pr(\overline{X} \le 19.9)$, and since the sampling distribution is approximately normal, we can find this area by computing the z-value:

$$z = \frac{\bar{x} - \mu}{\sigma_{\bar{x}}} = \frac{19.9 - 20}{0.05} = -2.00.$$

   Looking in table 3.14 we find that $\Pr(Z \le -2) = \Pr(Z \ge 2) = 1 - 0.9772 = 0.0228$. Thus, if the population mean is indeed $\mu = 20$ ounces and the population standard deviation $\sigma = 0.5$ ounces, the probability that the consumer group's test will result in a sample mean less than 19.9 ounces is rather small.

24.   a) The least squares line is given by $\hat{y} = 20.0287 + 0.6624x$, where the notation $\hat{y}$ denotes predicted or estimated y. The coefficient of determination of the regression, R^2, is 0.3978, which means that the explanatory variable, x, explains approximately 39.78% of the variation in y.

   b) The least squares line would be upward sloping (slope=0.6624).

25. The hypothesis test is set as follows:

$H_0: b = 0$

$H_1: b > 0$.

Analyzing the regression output of figure 3.28 we find that the p-value of the variable x is 0.0007. This number is smaller than 0.01 (1%), so, this means we can reject the null hypothesis in favor of the alternative at a significance level of 1%.

CHAPTER 4

TEST YOUR UNDERSTANDING 1

The information given tells us the following:

$$500 \times e^{0.06t} = 800,$$

and we need to solve for t. So, first divide both sides by 500 and then apply natural logarithms to get:

$$\ln(e^{0.06t}) = \ln(1.60)$$
$$0.06t = \ln(1.60)$$
$$t = \frac{\ln(1.60)}{0.06}$$
$$t = 7.8 \text{ years.}$$

TEST YOUR UNDERSTANDING 2

(1) An annuity pays a fixed sum each year for a specified number of years, while a perpetuity pays a fixed sum each year forever.

(2) First, let's draw a time line of the situation:

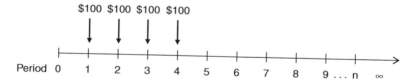

We can view this payment stream as the difference between two perpetuities: one starting at $t = 0$ (first payment at $t = 1$) minus one starting at $t = 4$ (first payment at $t = 5$).

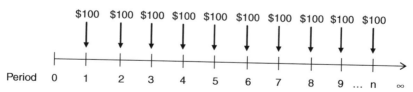

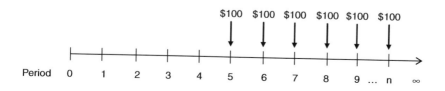

The present value of a perpetuity that starts $t = 0$ is

$$\text{PV perpetuity}_0 = \frac{100}{0.10} = 1,000.$$

The present value of a perpetuity that starts $t = 4$ is

$$\text{PV} = \$1,000 \times \left[\frac{1}{(1 + 0.10)^4} \right] = \$683.01.$$

So, the present value of the annuity is $\$1,000 - \$683.01 = \$316.99$.
We can now verify our result using the annuity formula of equation (4.5):

$$\text{PV of annuity} = \$100 \times \left[\frac{1}{0.10} - \frac{1}{0.10(1 + .010)^4} \right]$$

$$= \$100 \times 3.1699 = \$316.99.$$

TEST YOUR UNDERSTANDING 3

(1) $E(r_p) = (0.5 \times 5) + (0.5 \times 9.8) = 7.4\%$.
(2) Table A.5 summarizes the reward and risk of the two alternatives.

Table A.5 Portfolios (Percentages)

Portfolio	Expected Return	Standard Deviation
Half in stock H	11.6	2.33
Half in T-bills	7.4	2.33

A portfolio that has half in stock H clearly dominates one that has half in T-bills. The half in stock H portfolio offers higher expected return with the *same* standard deviation as the half T-bill portfolio.

TEST YOUR UNDERSTANDING 4

If $\beta_i = 0$, then the appropriate rate of return of stock i is the risk-free rate. You can see this by substituting in the formula:

$$r_i = r_f + 0(r_m - r_f)$$

$$r_i = r_f.$$

PRACTICE EXERCISES

1. $PV = \frac{2,800}{(1+0.08)^2} = \$2,400.55$.

2. The maximum you would be willing to pay for this asset is the present value, which is

$$PV = \frac{3,000}{(1 + 0.09)^2} = \$2,525.04.$$

3. $FV = 1,000 \times (1 + 0.045)^3 = \$1,141.17.$
4. $FV = 800 \times (1 + 0.05)^5 = \$1,021.03.$
5. $PV_A = 1,000 + \frac{2,300}{1+0.15} = \$3,000$ and $PV_B = \frac{3,400}{1+0.15} = \$2,956.52.$
   Since $PV_A > PV_B$, project A is better.
6. $PV_A = \frac{50,000}{1.07} + \frac{60,000}{1.07^2} + \frac{70,000}{1.07^3} = \$156,276.15,$

$$PV_B = \frac{60,000}{1.07} + \frac{60,000}{1.07^2} + \frac{60,000}{1.07^3} = \$157,458.96, \quad \text{and}$$

$$PV_C = \frac{70,000}{1.07} + \frac{60,000}{1.07^2} + \frac{50,000}{1.07^3} = \$158,641.78.$$

Project C is the best project because its present value is higher than the present value of the other two projects.

7. $S = 1,000 \left(1 + \frac{0.08}{4}\right)^{1.5 \times 4} = \$1,126.16.$
8. First, we compute the rate of inflation

$$\pi = \frac{105 - 100}{100} = 0.05 = 5.0\%.$$

Then, we use this result to calculate the real interest rate as follows:

$$1 + r = \frac{1 + 0.126}{1 + 0.05} = \frac{1.126}{1.05} = 1.072.$$

Solving for r we get:

$$r = 1.072 - 1 = 7.2\%.$$

(With the approximation formula you get $r \approx 12.6 - 5 = 7.6\%$).

9. a. $r_e = \left(1 + \frac{0.136}{2}\right)^2 - 1 = 0.1406 = 14.06\%.$
   b. $r_e = \left(1 + \frac{0.134}{4}\right)^4 - 1 = 0.1409 = 14.09\%.$
   c. $r_e = \left(1 + \frac{0.135}{12}\right)^{12} - 1 = 0.1437 = 14.37\%.$ This is the preferred option.
10. PV annuity $= 100 \times \left[\frac{1}{0.05} - \frac{1}{0.05(1+0.05)^{10}}\right] = 100 \times [20 - 12.28] = \$772.$
11. PV of perpetuity $= \frac{100}{0.05} = \$2,000.$

12. To get the annual payment we use the annuity formula:

$$C = \frac{11,245}{\left[\frac{1}{0.10} - \frac{1}{0.10(1+0.10)^4}\right]} = \$3547.41.$$

Table A.6 contains the amortization schedule for this loan.

Table A.6 Amortization Schedule (Dollars)

Year	Principal Outstanding at Beginning of Period	Interest per Period	Periodic Payment	Amortization of Loan	Principal Outstanding at End of Period
1	11,245.00	1,124.50	3,547.47	2,422.97	8,822.03
2	8,822.03	882.20	3,547.47	2,665.27	6,156.76
3	6,156.76	615.68	3,547.47	2,931.79	3,224.97
4	3,224.97	322.50	3,547.47	3,224.97	0.00

13. PV of growing perpetuity $= \frac{100}{0.05-0.01} = \frac{100}{0.04} = \$2,500.00$.

14. $PV = \frac{10}{(1.05)^2} + \frac{20}{(1.05)^4} = \$25.52$.

15. $NPV = -11,000 + \frac{3,000}{1.08} + \frac{4,000}{(1.08)^2} + \frac{5,000}{(1.08)^3} = -\$823.71$. No, the manager should not buy the machine since the net present value is negative.

16. The expected cash flow of the project is $0.5 \times 2,100 + 0.5 \times 100 = \$1,100$.

So, the NPV of this project is:
$NPV = -1,000 + \frac{1,100}{(1.08)^2} = -1,000 + 943.07 = -\$56.93 < 0$. You should not invest in the project since the net present value is negative.

17. Let's compare how much the washing machine costs in today's dollars in the three stores.

Store A: $600

Store B: $PV = \frac{625}{(1.05)} = \$595.24$

Store C: $PV = 200 + \frac{110}{(1.05)} + \frac{110}{(1.05)^2} + \frac{110}{(1.05)^3} + \frac{110}{(1.05)^4} = \$590.05$.

So, even though it appears that Store C charges the highest price ($640), with the payment plan this is the store that offers the best deal.

18. a. $100 \times \left[\frac{1}{0.05} - \frac{1}{0.05(1+0.05)^{30}}\right] + \frac{1,000}{(1+0.05)^{30}} = 1,537.25 + 231.38$
$= \$1,768.62$.

b. $100 \times \left[\frac{1}{0.10} - \frac{1}{0.10(1+0.10)^{30}}\right] + \frac{1,000}{(1+0.10)^{30}} = 942.69 + 57.31$
$= \$1,000.00$.

c. $100 \times \left[\frac{1}{0.15} - \frac{1}{0.15(1+0.15)^{30}}\right] + \frac{1,000}{(1+0.15)^{30}} = 656.60 + 15.10$
$= \$671.70$.

d. An inverse relationship between interest rates and bond prices. As interest rates rise, the price of the bond falls.

19. $50 \times \left[\frac{1}{0.06} - \frac{1}{0.06(1+0.06)^{12}} \right] + \frac{1,000}{(1+0.06)^{12}} = (50 \times 8.38) + 496.97 =$ $916.16.

20. $80 \times \left[\frac{1}{0.05} - \frac{1}{0.05(1+0.05)^{20}} \right] + \frac{1,000}{(1+0.05)^{20}} = (80 \times 12.46) + 340.46 = \$$ $1,373.87$.

21. $40 \times \left[\frac{1}{0.05} - \frac{1}{0.05(1+0.05)^{20}} \right] + \frac{1,000}{(1+0.05)^{20}} = (40 \times 12.46) + 376.89 = \$$ 875.38.

22. $P_0 = \frac{5}{0.085-0.02} = \$76.92$.

23. First we calculate the expected return of each stock:

$$E(r_K) = (0.5 \times 7) + (0.5 \times 18) = 12.5\%,$$
$$E(r_Q) = (0.5 \times 10.5) + (0.5 \times 3.5) = 7\%.$$

Now, we can calculate the expected return of the portfolio:

$$E(r_p) = (0.7 \times 12.5) + (0.3 \times 7) = 10.85\%.$$

To get the variance of the portfolio, we first calculate the variance of each stock:

$$\sigma_K^2 = [0.5 \times (7 - 12.5)^2] + [0.5 \times (18 - 12.5)^2] = 30.25,$$
$$\sigma_Q^2 = [0.5 \times (10.5 - 7)^2] + [0.5 \times (3.5 - 7)^2] = 12.25.$$

Then, we calculate the covariance between the returns of the two stocks:

$$\sigma_{KQ} = [0.5 \times (7 - 12.5) \times (10.5 - 7)]$$
$$+ [0.5 \times (18 - 12.5) \times (3.5 - 7)] = -19.25.$$

Now, we can calculate the variance of the portfolio:

$$\sigma_p^2 = (0.7^2 \times 30.25) + (0.3^2 \times 12.25) + (2 \times 0.7 \times 0.3 \times -19.25)$$
$$= 7.84.$$

The standard deviation of the portfolio is:

$$\sigma_p = \sqrt{7.84} = 2.8\%.$$

24. First we need to compute the expected return of stock M:

$$E(r_M) = 0.45 \times 3 + 0.55 \times 13 = 8.5\%.$$

Now, we can calculate the expected return of the portfolio:

$$E(r_p) = 0.60 \times 8.5 + 0.40 \times 5.5 = 7.3\%.$$

To get the standard deviation we first calculate the variance of stock M:

$$\sigma_M^2 = \left(0.45 \times [3 - 8.5]^2\right) + (0.55 \times [13 - 8.5]^2) = 24.75.$$

Next, the standard deviation:

$$\sigma_M = \sqrt{24.75} = 4.97\%.$$

Now, we can calculate the standard deviation of the portfolio:

$$\sigma_p = 0.60 \times 4.97 = 2.98\%.$$

25. We know that $15 = 4.5 + (\beta_Z \times 7.5)$. So, solving for beta we get that $\beta_Z = 1.4$.

Notes

I   Business Math: Functions and Graphs

1. This rule is equivalent to adding or subtracting the same number to both sides of the equation.
2. The symbol ∞ (read "infinity") is not a number. When we write $[b, \infty)$, we are referring to the interval starting at b and continuing indefinitely to the right. Likewise, the symbol $-\infty$ (read "minus infinity") denotes an interval continuing indefinitely to the left. Note that we never write $(b, \infty]$ or $[-\infty, b)$.
3. If x is a negative number, then its absolute value is the number that remains when the sign is removed. For example, the absolute value of -3 is 3. To denote absolute value we use the symbol $||$. Note that $|a|$ can never be negative.
4. You can find the rules that apply to negative numbers in Appendix A.
5. You can find the rules that apply to fractions in Appendix A.
6. A way to verify if an equation defines a function is by drawing a vertical line in the graph of the function. An equation specifies a function if each vertical line passes through at most one point on the graph of the equation (this is known as the *vertical-line test for a function*).
7. In some cases, however, there are multiple solutions and sometimes none at all.
8. This method is called the *substitution method*.
9. A price index such as the CPI, which uses a *base-period fixed consumption basket*, is called a Laspeyres index. Another common type of price index is the Paasche index that, instead, uses the *current year's basket*. Both, Laspeyres and Paasche, are fixed-weight price indexes, that is, the quantities of the various goods and services in each index remain unchanged. For the Laspeyres index, however, the quantities remain unchanged at *base-year levels* and for the Paasche index, they remain unchanged at *current-year levels*.

2   Business Math: Optimization

1. Section 1.7 reviews these properties of functions.
2. For the more general case where the function is given by $f(x) = g(h(x))$, the derivative rule is $f'(x) = g'(h(x))h'(x)$.
3. We require $b > 0$ to avoid imaginary numbers (e.g., $(-2)^{1/2} = \sqrt{-2} = i\sqrt{2}$) and exclude $b = 1$ since $f(x) = 1^x = 1$.
4. For more detail on compound interest see section 4.3.
5. "Rule 69" is a nice shortcut to calculate doubling-times with continuously compounded interest rates. The rule says that with continuous compounding, the time that it takes for the investment to double is $t = \dfrac{69.3}{\text{interest rate in percent}}$.
   Using the numbers in our example, we get $t = \dfrac{69.3}{5} = 13.9$.

6. For the more general case where the exponent of e is a function $u(x)$, that is, $f(x) = e^{u(x)}$, the derivative rule is $f'(x) = e^{u(x)} u'(x)$.
7. For the more general case where the function is given by exponent of $f(x) = \ln u(x)$, the derivative rule is $f'(x) = \frac{u'(x)}{u(x)}$.
8. I do not cover integration in this book since I believe this is not a tool required in any of the typical quantitative MBA courses.
9. I have taken a shortcut that could be problematic if one were to do a more formal analysis. The area under the demand curve measures the consumer surplus only if income effects can be ignored. Otherwise, we need to use a *compensated demand curve* (a demand curve built up from substitution effects only) to measure it. However, this is not a problem unless we are looking at purchases that account for a large share of the consumer's income; for example, housing or cars.
10. The good in this example is a normal good.

3   STATISTICAL ANALYSIS PRIMER

1. Suppose that our data set constitutes the entire population. In this case, we could use the formula for the population variance, σ^2, which is defined as

$$\sigma^2 = \frac{\sum\limits_{i=i}^{n} (x_i - \mu)^2}{n}.$$

Note that in the population variance formula, the denominator is n instead of $(n-1)$. A terse explanation for the difference in the denominators of the formulas of the sample and the population variance is that when we calculate s^2 the deviations are taken from the sample mean $\bar{x}$ and not from the population mean μ. This introduces a downward bias in the deviations. To create an *unbiased estimator* of σ^2, the formula for the sample variance has $(n-1)$ in the denominator rather than n.

2. Remember that random variables are typically denoted with capital letters and particular values of the variables with lowercase letters. So, once we sample from the population and obtain a value of $\overline{X}$, we will have obtained a *particular* sample mean, which we denote by $\bar{x}$ (e.g., $\bar{x} = 13.89$).
3. Section 1.9.2 reviews index numbers.

4   MATHEMATICS OF FINANCE

1. The stated interest rate is also known as the "annual percentage rate" or "APR."
2. I will consider only the case of fixed payments (i.e., annuities).
3. If the cash flows start this period (i.e., at $t = 0$), the formula for the present value of the perpetuity is:

$$\text{PV perpetuity} = C + \frac{C}{r}.$$

4. Since the perpetuity is worth $1,000 at period 4, we are indifferent between receiving a lump sum of $1,000 at period 4 and receiving a perpetuity with a first payment occurring in period 5. Receiving a lump sum of $1,000 in period 4 allows us to set up a perpetuity in which the first payment is received in period 5.

5. Section 3.8.1 reviews the concept of expected value.

REFERENCES

Abel B., and B. S. Bernanke, *Macroeconomics*, 5th ed., Pearson Addison Wesley, 2005.

Albright S., W. L. Winston, and C. J. Zappe, *Data Analysis for Managers*, 2nd ed., Brooks/Cole – Thomson Learning, 2004.

Besanko A., and R. R. Braeutigam, *Microeconomics*, 2nd ed., John Wiley & Sons, 2005.

Bodie Z., A. Kane, and A. J. Marcus, *Investments*, 6th ed., McGraw-Hill/Irwin, 2005.

Brealey R. A., S. C. Myers, and F. Allen, *Principles of Corporate Finance*, 8th ed., McGraw-Hill, 2006.

Casella G., and R. L. Berger, *Statistical Inference*, Duxbury Press, 1990.

Haessler F., R. Paul, and R. Wood, *Introductory Mathematical Analysis for Business Economics and the Life and Social Sciences*, 11th ed., Pearson Prentice Hall, 2005.

Jehle G. A., and P. J. Reny, *Advanced Microeconomic Theory*, 2nd ed., Addison Wesley, 2001.

Mas-Colell, M. D. Whinston, and J. R. Green, *Microeconomic Theory*, Oxford University Press, 1995.

Pindyck R. S., and D. L. Rubinfeld, *Microeconomics*, 6th ed., Pearson Prentice Hall, 2005.

Ross S. A., R. W. Westerfield, and J. Jaffe, *Corporate Finance*, 7th ed., McGraw-Hill/Irwin, 2005.

Varian H. R., *Intermediate Microeconomics: A Modern Approach*, 5th ed., W.W.Norton & Company, 1999.

Zimmerman J. L., *Accounting for Decision Making and Control*, 5th ed., McGraw-Hill, 2006.

Index

absolute value, 14, 193
aggregate production function, 38
alternative hypothesis, 121–3
amortization, 139–40
annuity, 139, 142, 146

balance sheet, 77
base, 33, 70–1
base period, 39–40
beta, 155–7
bonds, 131, 146–7
  zero-coupon, 148–9
budget constraint, 21–4, 31–2, 67
budget set, 22

capital, 33, 36, 38
capital asset pricing model
  (CAPM), 156
Cartesian plane, 4
Central Limit Theorem, 113–14
ceteris paribus, 60
chance nodes, 104
choice variables, 66
Cobb-Douglas function, 33–5, 38
coefficient, 7, 18
  of determination, 118
comparative statics analysis, 79
concave function, 45, 56, 62
constant-growth (or Gordon) model,
  149
constant returns to scale, 36
constants, 7–9, 47–8, 59, 84
constraint, 66, 68
Consumer Price Index (CPI), 39–40,
  193
consumer surplus, 74, 76, 194
consumption baskets, 21–2
continuous function, 30–1, 52, 73
convex function, 45, 56, 63
correlation coefficient, 154–5
  population, 95
  sample, 94–6
cost function, 49–50
coupon, 146–8
  rate, 147–8

covariance, 93–6, 152, 154, 156
cumulative distribution function
  (cdf), 99

debt security, 146
decision tree, 103–5
demand, 3
  curve, 5–6, 9–10, 17–18, 60, 74–6,
    79, 194
  function, 4–5, 9–10, 61
  linear, 9
  market, 27–8
derivatives, 31, 47–50, 53–5, 57, 62–6,
  68, 73
  partial, 59–60
  second, 55, 58, 62–6
descriptive statistics, 83
deviations, 92, 94, 101, 194
differentiable function, 31, 51
discount rate, 132, 139–40,
  142–3, 146
  risk-adjusted, 145
discounted cash flow, 144
distributions, 88–9, 91
  bimodal, 89
  skewed to the left (or negatively
    skewed), 90–1
  skewed to the right (or positively
    skewed), 89
  symmetric, 88
diversification, 154–5
dividends, 149–50

endogenous variable, 76, 79
equations, 7, 19, 26, 68, 116
  explicit, 8–9
  implicit, 8
equilibrium, 76, 79
  market, 28–9, 79
estimator, 113, 194
exogenous variable, 76, 79
expected cash flow, 145
expected return, 145, 150, 153, 157
expected value, 100–1, 103
exponential function, 69–72

exponents, 33, 35, 48, 55, 70–1, 73
 fractional, 34, 48

face value, 146, 148–9
finance charge, 140
first-order condition, 62, 68–9
fitted values, 117
flow variables, 77
frequency table, 87–9
functions, 1–2, 4–5, 119
 linear, 7–8, 45–6
 multivariate, 3
 nonlinear, 45–6, 50
future value, 133, 136

general linear form, 20
gross domestic product (GDP), 77–9
growth accounting equation, 38
growth rate, 37, 142, 149

histogram, 87–91
homogenous function, 35
horizontal axis (or x-axis), 4, 7, 13, 70,
 73, 119
horizontal intercept (or x-intercept),
 13–14, 18, 21, 24–5
horizontal line, 25

income, 3–4, 22–4, 60, 67–8, 79
 elasticity, 60–1
income statement, 77
index, 34
 number, 39, 119
 price, 39
inequalities, 10–11
inferences, 83, 92, 112–13
inferior good, 60
inflation, 39, 134
interest, 131, 149
 compound, 70, 135
 continuously compounded, 71, 73,
  136, 193
 simple, 70, 135
interest rate, 131, 147
 effective, 137–8
 nominal, 134
 real, 134
 stated, 137–8, 194
interval notation, 11

kink, 30–1

labor, 33, 36, 38, 52–3
Lagrange multipliers, 67–8
Lagrangian function, 67, 69

least squares estimation, 117–18
least squares line, 118–19
logarithms, 71–2
 common, 71
 natural, 71–3, 137

marginal cost, 49–50
marginal functions, 49
marginal product of labor, 52–3
marginal utility, 57–8
 diminishing, 58
maximum, 45, 61, 64, 66
mean, 85–6, 88–91, 100, 107–8, 145
 population, 85, 113, 115, 194
 sample, 85, 113–15, 194
median, 85–6, 88–91
minimum, 45, 61, 63–4, 66
mode, 87–91
model, 76, 83
monotonic function, 31

nominal variable, 77
normal distribution, 107, 109, 113
normal good, 60, 194
null hypothesis, 121–3

objective function, 61, 66–7
optimization, 45, 61
 constrained, 62, 66–7
 unconstrained, 61, 67–8
outlier, 86

p-value, 122–3
paired variables, 93
perpetuity, 140–2, 194–5
 growing, 142, 149
population, 83, 89, 112–13
portfolio, 150–5
 expected return of, 151, 153
 standard deviation of, 152–4
 variance of, 152, 154–5
power function, 33, 70
present value, 132, 139–44, 147
 net (NPV), 143–5, 158
price, 2–7, 31, 60, 76
 of alternative goods, 3–4, 60, 79
 of inputs, 4, 79
 of technologically related goods, 4, 79
price-taker, 28
principal, 70, 131, 139
probability, 83, 97–9, 104, 108–9, 145
 cumulative, 99
 density function (pdf), 106
 distribution, 98, 100, 103, 107, 113
profit function, 65

quantity demanded, 3, 7, 60
quantity supplied, 4

radical, 34
random error, 116
random variables, 98, 113, 194
   continuous, 106–8
   discrete, 98–102
rate of change, 12, 47, 77
real variable, 77
regression, 115, 119
   coefficients, 116, 120, 122
   output, 118–19, 123
reservation price, 74
residuals, 117–18
revenue function, 2
risk-free interest rate, 145, 152, 156
risk premium, 145, 156

sample, 83, 113
   statistic, 113
sampling distribution, 113–14
scatterplot, 93, 95, 115, 119, 124
second-order condition, 62
security market line, 156
sigma (or summation) notation, 84
significance level, 121
simple linear regression, 115–19
slope, 5, 12–14, 17–21, 24–5, 30–2,
   45–7, 49–50, 53, 55–6, 58, 62–3,
   116, 120, 122–4, 147
slope-intercept form, 13
smooth function, 30–1, 52, 62–3
square root, 34

standard deviation, 101, 103, 108, 145,
   151
   population, 92
   sample, 92–3
standard normal variable, 108–9
stock variables, 77
stocks, 131, 149
supply, 4, 61, 79–80
   market, 27–8, 79
systematic risk (or market risk), 155

terms, 7, 9–10
time-series data, 119
Type I error, 121–2
Type II error, 121

unsystematic risk (or unique risk), 155
utility function, 57, 67–8

variables, 1, 7
   dependent, 1–4, 7, 12, 116–19, 122
   independent, 1–4, 7, 12, 73, 116, 118
variance, 100–1, 103, 107, 113, 118,
   145, 151, 156
   population, 92, 194
   sample, 92–3, 194
vertical axis (or y-axis), 4, 7, 13, 119
vertical intercept (or y-intercept),
   13–14, 17–21, 24–5
vertical line, 25

yield to maturity, 146–8

z-value, 108–9, 111, 114

Made in the USA
Lexington, KY
08 August 2011